Stefan Krneta was born in 1988 in Belgrade. He graduated from the Faculty of Business and Financial Studies in 2011. After graduation, he spent several years working as a director of an online retail company. He is interested in literature from the field of self-improvement, psychology, reading and learning.

Krneta Stefan

Speed Reading
A Complete Manual with Exercises

Read 200% to 300% faster while maintaining an excellent level of comprehension and memory.

Speed Reading – A Complete Manual with Exercises
Stefan Krneta

Cover design: Nataša Ristić

Publishing company "Korisna knjiga" d.o.o.
Beogradska 172
11224 Vrčin
Serbia
+381 (0)11 3463 072
+381 (0)60 3463 072
office@korisnaknjiga.com
www.korisnaknjiga.com

Year of publication: 2018

Reproduction, distribution, publication, modification or any other utilization of this copyrighted work or any of its parts is strictly prohibited in any scope or by any mean, including photocopying, printing and storing in electronic form. These actions are considered a copyright infringement.

Contents

Foreword 1

About speed reading 2

Preface 2
A Few Interesting Stats 3
The Effects of Speed Reading on Our Brain 5
What is your current record regarding the number of books read in one month? 7
The Incredible Effects of Reading on Our Lives 8
Benefits of Speed Reading 14
When was the speed reading concept established? ... 21
Test your reading speed! 25

Conditions You Need to Practice Speed Reading 31

Influence of work environment on concentration and speed reading 31
What time of day is the best for reading? 34
Food with positive effect on concentration 36
Influence of a healthy lifestyle on reading speed 45

Eye Exercises and How to Preserve Your Vision 46

Theoretical Part 48

Bad Reading Habits 48

Technique of Speed Reading with Visual Aid 55

Tips to Improve Comprehension Level 58

A few of the most beautiful quotes on motivation 61

Causes of Bad Concentration and Comprehension 63

Test you level of comprehension! 64

Punctuation marks and reading by segments 81

The power of peripheral vision 85

Advanced meta-guiding techniques 92

Exercises and Practice 105

Exercises for developing peripheral vision and perception
.. 105

Metronome as a reading aid 134

21-day exercise plan for developing and maintaining the reading speed 135

Set the goal - your desired reading speed 140

Bonus Chapter: How to Improve Your Memory? 142

The Journal of Achieved Results and for Progress Tracking 158

Author's afterword 160

Literature: 161

Disclaimer 164

Notes 165

Foreword

I first got interested in speed reading while I was still in high school. It was some 10 years ago. That was the first time I read a book "Speed Reading" written by Tony Buzan. After reading his advices, I started developing an entirely different perspective on reading. Not only I improved my reading speed, but I also started enjoying the books that I read more. In the last couple of years, I spent a lot of time reading and learning. Since in the meantime I forgot most of the speed reading techniques, I decided to refresh my knowledge.

After reading just three books from the field, I became very interested in the subject. With each new book about speed reading I developed a deeper knowledge about the topic. After reading some 15 books, attending several courses and gaining some experience, I decided to collect all this knowledge in a single document. As the number of my tips continued to grow and reached more than 100 pages, I decided to organize the material and publish it in this book. This was my attempt to create a quick reference guide to keep at hand at any time.

I think that speed reading is a very useful skill. It helped me improve my reading speed by 2-3 times after just a few weeks of practice. I hope it will help you improve your reading speed, as well.

Author: Stefan Krneta - Vrčin 16.3.2018

About speed reading

Preface

Did you know that there are readers that can read 4-5 times faster than other people? Speed reading World Record holder Anne Jones is capable of reading a 759-page book in just 47 minutes! Just imagine what would your everyday life be, if you mastered the speed reading techniques!

How about reading a new book every day? Do you think it's impossible? It's not. It is only a matter of being persistent and making an effort to perfect appropriate speed reading techniques.

Being an average reader, I was able to read one new book each month. Eventually, through hard work I managed to change my habits and began reading five books a month. Thus I reached a maximum number of books that could be read by an average reader in a month (if reading 2 hours a day).

The aim of this book is to introduce you to speed reading methods and techniques. The book has four main segments, each one of them answering one of the following questions:

1. What do you need to know about speed reading?
(Useful information, curiosities and facts)

2. What requirements you must meet to successfully use the speed reading techniques?
(tips for maximizing efficiency)

3. What reading techniques exist and how to apply them?
(detailed explanation on use of speed reading techniques)

4. What are the best exercises to improve reading speed?
(detailed 21-day program of 20-minute daily exercises)

The first three units contain useful tips and give detailed description of existing speed reading techniques and how they are used. The last segment contains just the exercises that are done once or more times a day, depending on the time you have available. Readers who lack patience to go through the theory and tips can start with the exercises right away, although I wouldn't recommend that.
The best results and the quickest progress are achieved, if you read this book in the order it was written.

A Few Interesting Stats

1. Did you know that 85% of all information is obtained through reading? Even the persons that don't have a habit of reading books are constantly required to read in their everyday life. Newspapers, various leaflets and instructions, subtitles – an average person is constantly required to read various texts.

2. In the recent years, the amount of available knowledge has grown by 30% every year. The best way to advance your private life and career is to read new and current books.

Self-improvement and collection of new information through everyday reading are preconditions for improvement. A person who doesn't spend at least an hour a day on personal improvement and acquiring new skills can't expect to have any success in private or professional life. The aim of this book, besides teaching about speed reading techniques, is to help you gain a habit of spending at least one hour a day on reading useful literature.

3. It's a little-known fact that even the most prestigious universities teach their students the speed reading techniques. Some of these universities include: *Harvard, Yale, Princeton, MIT, New York University, Fordham, Stanford.* Such renowned institutions have over time became aware of the importance of speed reading, so they started teaching their students the proper techniques very early during their studies.

4. If you improve your reading speed by just 25%, you will be able to save 10 days a year, provided you read two hours a day. The aim of this book is to help you increase your reading speed by 2-3 times by the end of the course. Average readers are capable of achieving this speed even after just three weeks of practice. Just look at the time you can save every year. Let's say you read one book a week. That makes for 48 books a year. If you increase your reading speed by two or three times you will be able to read 96 to 144 books over the same time period.

5. The wealthiest and the most successful people on average spend two to three hours a day on reading books and self-improvement. How much time a day do you spend on reading and on your education?

The Effects of Speed Reading on Our Brain

According to the latest research, an average brain is capable to process 800 to 1000 words per minute. Considering this, an average reading speed of 200 words per minute seems a bit low. You are probably wondering what mistakes we make when we read. What makes a fast reader different from an average one? You'll find detailed answers to these questions in the third part of the book which contains a detailed explanation of reading techniques. Let me just mention that the fastest readers in the world can achieve reading speed of up to 3000 words per minute.

Knowing these facts, it doesn't sound unusual that we are unable to concentrate when reading at a speed of 200 words per minute. In other words, our brain gets bored. You have probably noticed that when reading your mind often starts wondering. More particularly, your brain feels relaxed, so it becomes hard to focus on reading and remembering the text you have read.

I'll give you an example.
Let's say you are given a task of carrying a bag of cement through a busy street in a city centre. The bag weighs 30 kg, so you will most certainly try to find the shortest way to get

the job done. In this example, it means 10 minutes of your time.

On the other side, your friend is given a task of carrying an empty bucket to the same place your bag is currently located. After 20 minutes, your friend carrying a bucket finally arrives at the destination. When asked what took him so long, he gave you the following explanations:
– I noticed some very nice shoe shops, so I took some time to look around;
– I met a childhood friend, so I stopped for a quick chat;
– I received an important text message that I had to reply to immediately;
– While passing by cafe I heard a song that I hadn't heard in 10 years, so stopped for a while to listen.

As you can see, when you are not 100% committed to a task, your mind starts wandering. The person who carried the heavy load had no time for anything else other than completing the task. It's the same thing with reading. If you use only 20% of your capacities, your mind starts wandering and you start having problems focusing.

By the way, in case you didn't know, the reading process itself has a beneficial effect on our brain. Scientists from Emory University in USA have found that reading strengthens connections between neurons and incites permanent positive neurological changes in the brain.

Here's what professor Gregory Berns, the lead author of the study, has to say on this subject:

"The neural changes that we found associated with physical sensation and movement systems suggest that reading a novel can transport you into the body of the protagonist."

"We already knew that good stories can put you in someone else's shoes in a figurative sense. Now we're seeing that something may also be happening biologically."

It has also been proven that reading serves as a great prevention against Alzheimer's disease, it reduces stress, improves positive thinking and helps us create friendly relationships more easily.

What is your current record regarding the number of books read in one month?

You have probably heard more than a few times that reading is important. Have you ever had the chance to experience the difference yourself? Did you try to dedicate one month just to reading? I suggest you try that and set a new record in the number of books read in one month. It may be 3 or 10 books, it really doesn't matter. What matters is that you make progress and feel proud of yourself and the number of books you read.

In time, when you develop a habit of reading a lot, you'll notice some changes. The way in which you see yourself and your environment will change. The contact with new books and information you acquire from them will make you start thinking differently. Your goals, desires and plans will start to change. Besides becoming capable of better expressing yourself, you'll also become wittier.

When I first started, I used to read one new book a month. As the time passed, I started replacing the books written in Serbian with German and English literature. In my opinion, the easiest way to learn a foreign language is to read a lot of books. Since I had the opportunity to see that on my own example, I decided to read even more and increased the number of books read a month to five. Very quickly, after just a few months of reading, I had no problem passing B2 level tests in German.

At the time, I had a wish to one day be able to write books in English and German. At the time I thought that everything that stood between me and my goal were some 200-300 books and C2 Level. Driven by this thought, I started exploring the ways to improve my reading speed. After reading about 15 books about speed reading, and after completing several courses and improving my knowledge through research I conducted myself, I decided to present all the information I collected in this manual.

The Incredible Effects of Reading on Our Lives

Reading has always been a special experience for me. The mere chance to learn about the ways of some of the greatest minds and to look the world through their eyes was something that I was always interested in. A vast selection of books being available now gives us more possibilities than ever before to find new information and to have a better view on different areas of our lives. In my

opinion, we can learn a lot by reading books written by people who have achieved great success in private, professional and social life. Also, by applying their advice we can even expect to achieve something similar. The quality of my life has significantly improved since I started to regularly read books. By reading five books a month I was able to significantly improve my knowledge from the fields I found interesting:
– development of useful daily routines and lose of bad habits;
– importance of healthy diet and regular exercises;
– psychology, communication and human relations;
– business organisation and company management.

I was also capable to conceive the importance of the concept of everyday self-improvement.

All the new knowledge I acquired over time lead to the extremely positive changes in my life, such as:
– easier and faster accomplishment of goals set;
– more energy and better physical condition;
– more free time, ability to spend one hour at work instead of six hours due to being able to better organize my schedule;
– higher income;
– many new ideas, plans and goals created using the inspiration found in new and interesting books;
– a sense of purpose, higher self-esteem;
– being able to dedicate myself to interests I previously had no time for.

Since I found that my five-books-a-month routine was the reason behind all these positive changes, I started thinking

how would my life look if I could read one new book every day.
So, if the fastest reader in the world can read an entire book in one hour, why couldn't I read a book in three or four hours? By following this logic, I started researching existing speed reading techniques and after a few months of practice I met my goal of reading 15 new books during one month. I didn't spend more than two hours a day reading.

The feeling a person starts to develop when he reads a lot is best described by this quote:

"A mind that is stretched by a new experience can never go back to its old dimensions." Oliver Wendell Holmes

My advice for beginners is to test themselves to find out how many new books they can read during one month. This number will be an interesting initial indicator that you can later compare with your new monthly record. If you have no idea where to start from, I recommend you to check out the following list of books.

My 10 Recommended Books

The Winning Principle – Bryan Tracy

Principle of Power – Anthony Robbins

The Art of the Good Life – Rolf Dobelli

The Why Cafe – John Strelecky

The Carpet Makers – Andreas Eschbach

QualityLand – Marc Uwe Kling

The Remains of the Day – Kazuo Ishiguro

The Pigeon - Patrick Süskind

A Man Called Ove - Fredrik Backman

The Hundred-Year-Old Man Who Climbed Out the Window and Disappeared - Jonas Jonasson

I think these are the books that everyone will like, so I can certainly recommend them.

I noticed an interesting thing - every new book makes us richer for one new experience. During his lifetime a man usually doesn't have the opportunity to visit certain places, meet interesting people or learn less known, but interesting facts. That's exactly what reading allows us to do. Each book has something that makes it special and different from the others. Sometimes it's a new idea or experience of the author that can change the way we see the world. And there are books for which people say that they changed their lives. I was sceptical myself when it came to this overly used phrase, but my scepticism was gone when I read the book: *Changing Habits - new everyday habits for success*, written by *Sjard Roscher*. This book was a turning point in my life. If I hadn't bumped into this book, I would probably stay on the expressway to average and boring life. In this book the author talks about the idea of replacing one bad habit with one good habit every month. On annual level, it means that we will gain 12 new good habits and lose 12 bad habits. When apply this advice for several years in a row, I think that you come very close to fulfilling the idea of perfect, fulfilled and good life.

However, let's get to the subject I'm writing about. In my experience, each book we read contains some useful information. Sum of useful information helps us lead a better life.

By the way, you can only read a limited number of books in a lifetime. No matter how fast someone reads, each individual can read only a limited number of new books. Ralf Dobolli described this nicely in his book *The Art of the Good Life*. Here's a metaphor he used: "Imagine having a big roll of tram tickets. One ticket is for one ride. The roll has certain length and therefore has a definite number of tickets. With every new book you read, you cancel one ticket, so it can no longer be used." Ralf's view on reading had a huge impact on me, so I started spending more time on choosing the books I wanted to read. Before that, I usually spent about five minutes on choosing a new book, but now I spend up to three times longer. Simply put, if you plan to spend an hour or more on reading a book, make sure that it is a good one. If you make a mistake and you don't like the book, don't read it. Some people are ready to force themselves to use a product or service to the maximum extent just because of its high price. In my opinion, if a purchased product or service doesn't prove to be useful, then there's no point in losing any time on it. This logic also applies to books. Every so often everyone makes a bad choice. The biggest mistake, in my opinion, is staying on the wrong path. So, try not to lose time on books that don't meet your expectations. Just choose another one. By the way, don't forget that your time is precious and treat it that way.

Here's an advice you may find interesting and useful. Keep records or journal about the books you read during a month. The journal should have 12 pages. One page for each month. You need the following columns:
– date on which you finished reading a book;
– book title;
– your rating (1 to 5);
– number of pages.

The journal will give you a nice visual overview of the books you have read sorted by date. You can also conveniently sum the number of pages of the books you have read and calculate the total number of pages.

You can use rating to choose the best book of each month. Each month you can select one book to be "the book of the month". I started a small tradition, so every January I read all the previous winners - the books that won "My Book of the Month" award during the previous year. :)

You should try this system on yourself. It will motivate you to keep trying, you will have a nice overview of the results you accomplished and a list of the best books you read so far.

Regarding the rereading of books, I noticed that certain people have problem with reading the same title again. They usually see it as a job they have already completed and which therefore carries no new information. I was of the same opinion when I started reading, but it changed over time. Now I think of book reading the same as as I think of listening to music. If I like a song, I will probably listen to it again. The same can be said for movies. Some books have to be read two or three times before they reveal their hidden meaning and show us what the author actually tried to say.

So, I think that certain books definitely deserve to be read more than once. Since people are prone to forgetting, we have one more reason to reread good books. Keeping this list can be very helpful for that cause.

I hope that this paragraph has, even just a little bit, sparked your will and desire to read. I, as the author of this book, will be satisfied if you read just one book a month more than usual. I believe that every step in the right direction, no matter how small it is, is beneficial in the long run.

Benefits of Speed Reading

Speed reading has many benefits. Many jobs and activities in life can benefit from our ability to quickly read and process new information. In this section, I will discuss just some of the areas of our lives that benefit the most from successful use of this skill.

How can speed reading help university students?

In this section I will give a few examples about the way in which speed reading facilitates and speeds up studying.

An average student reads a large number of books during studies. Some of the books have 1000 pages or even more. Let's assume that you have to study 6 hours a day to graduate from university. It's 2190 hours a year. If you could improve your reading speed by just 25%, on annual level you would save 527 hours or 22 days. These numbers look unreal when put in this perspective.

The aim of this book is to improve your reading speed by two or three times. Speaking from my previous experience, anyone can reach these speeds by applying appropriate techniques and with a little bit of practice. So, a student can expect to save 1095 hours a year provided he doubles his reading speed or 1460 hours if he learns to read three times faster. Speaking in days, he would save 45, i.e. 60 days a year. It sounds unbelievable, but numbers don't lie. it will take 3h on average to read this book + 20 minutes practice a day over three weeks, which means you will need 10 hours. So, if you invest 10 hours to improve your reading speed, you can expect to save from 1095 to 1460 hours a year, the time you can then use for other activities. When you put things in this perspective, an effort put into learning speed reading techniques is certainly justified. If you have just enrolled to university, I must confess that I envy you, because when I started my studies at the university I wasn't considered a fast reader. If I were, it would certainly be much more easier and pleasing for me to study and pass exams.

Effects of Speed Reading on Writers

The next example of positive benefits of speed reading can be seen in persons who decide to become writers and make their living from selling books. In order to be successful, an author must concentrate on two activities. A lot of reading and writing. And I mean every day, not only when he feels inspired or ready for work.

Everyday writing and reading gives the writer an opportunity to improve, to develop his style and to become better at writing. It very rarely happens in this line of work that a person without reading and writing habits becomes successful. One of the most famous writers of today, Steven King, in his memoires *On Writing* reveals that he reads seven new books a month on average and writes about 2000 words a day. Perhaps you didn't know, but fees of the bestselling writers can be pretty high. For example, if a book reaches the Amazon Best Sellers list, it can bring daily income of about 20000 euro or higher. As I see it, if you do the same things the best writers do, you can expect to achieve the same results after some time. Speed reading can prove to be a huge shortcut towards achieving the results in this field. If you set yourself a goal of reading and writing two to three times more than professional writers, then you can very soon expect to achieve the same results as them.

Effects of Speed Reading on Career

In his book *The Winning Principle* Brian Tracy states that a person needs seven years or 10000 hours to get into top 10% of the best and the most paid people in his line of work. He estimates that this is a time period you need to acquire new knowledge and skills required to successfully perform business tasks.

Now that we know that the period of learning and acquiring new knowledge is closely related to reading, we can see how useful it is to learn the speed reading techniques. Let's say for example that a person working in marketing reads one new book about marketing a month. It makes for 12 books a year, provided, of course, that this person spends at least a little bit of time on development of its professional skills. Many people stop improving their professional knowledge as soon as they find a job. Let's compare a person who works in marketing and reads one new book on the topic with a speed reader who reads 15 books a month on the same topic. The amount of knowledge, information and new ides acquired by a person who reads a lot is huge. This soon starts having effect on its performance. In my opinion, a person who becomes an expert, not only can expect to be better paid, but can also find a better job. The income then becomes several times higher than before. Let's see what happens with a person who spends time on education and continuous development over a long period of time. If such person works in marketing, it can expect to earn very large bonuses. For example, let's say that he presents a marketing idea to the company management and that such idea brings 100.000 euro profit to the company. He can expect 20.000 euro bonus. It is very common that persons who show exceptional performance get wealthy rewards. I am also a supporter of incentives based on performance.

The example I described above can easily be applied to any profession. In general, the faster you gain the required knowledge, the sooner you'll be in a position to have higher earnings, get better job and have more spare time. After a few years and several hundreds of books read, it is most likely that there will be no expert in the city or even in the country who is better than you.

Effects of Speed Reading on Our Ability to Make the Right Decisions

The decisions we make are mostly based on our previous experience. It often happens so that we don't have the experience in some fields and must guess the right decision. When we read books we are put into different situations and we have the opportunity to see how others behave in such situations. Reading and thinking about their actions often allows us to make our own conclusions and develop better ideas on how to approach certain problem or subject.

For example, imagine a person that wants to build a wooden, tree house. If it approaches this task without any experience or skills, it is quite possible that it will not be able to build the tree house at all. Not to mention concerns about safety of such structure. On the other hand, a person that spends free time reading books and instructions on building of environmentally-friendly wooden houses has a vast insight and gets a large amount of useful building advices. Also, it very often comes across advertisements of construction companies. The advertisements shown when a person does the Internet searches are profiled according to its interests. A person gets offered various discounts on materials, receives many useful information, etc.

After some time, an informed person acquires all the knowledge required to complete the project. Therefore, a person who reads a lot and gets informed can, as this example shows, make much better decisions regarding:
- selection of the best tree or building site
- legal procedure regarding construction of this object
- costs of the project
- duration of construction
- the best companies in the industry.

Therefore, it can be said that a person with a habit of reading a lot may use its knowledge to make much better decisions than the person without a reading habit. In professional literature, such advantage is often called an *unfair advantage*. In a way, person A and person B from this example can't compete with each other.

This example can be applied to almost any important decision you have to make. As a speed reader you have both the ability and time to read sufficient number of books from the field of interest and to acquire all the knowledge you need to make the right decision. A slow reader doesn't have the time to acquire sufficient knowledge and therefore often makes worse decisions. It is often said that good and fulfilled life is the sum of good decisions. Start making them. :)

Effects of Speed Reading on Fast Learning of Foreign Languages

Knowledge of foreign languages is very appreciated today. Individuals that speak several languages have more friends, better jobs and lead more interesting lives. In addition to all of that, it has been proven that learning foreign languages has positive effects on brain development. One of the best ways to learn a foreign language is to read books written in that language. You can start with children's books and later move on to more serious literature. The process of learning foreign words from a dictionary also becomes much faster and easier.

If you had previously found learning foreign languages difficult and tedious, you might notice how speed reading made it easy. You will not only improve your efficiency, focus and memory, but over time you will start to love this activity. In a separate part of the book, near the end, you can find a few advices about how speed reading makes language learning easier.
Besides the above, there is almost an indefinite number of other jobs and activities that benefit from speed reading.

To summarize, speed reading will allow you to:
– study with ease;
– develop your career faster;
– improve your ability to make the right decisions;
– learn foreign languages faster and more efficiently;
– become more eloquent and improve communication skills;

These are just some of the benefits that crossed my mind, but I believe there are many more. Don't forget that life is too short to have small goals and wishes.

In the following chapter, I'll talk about history of speed reading and list the pros and cons of attending a seminar.

When was the speed reading concept established?

The first speed reading school was opened in 1959 by *Evelyn Wood*. Even during her university years, *Evelyn* noticed that she was able to read quite fast. Being able to read 2700 words in a minute, she stood out from her friends and colleagues. After spending years on developing systems and techniques, as well as improving her reading speed, she became a university professor in Utah (USA). She is considered to be among the first professor that used part of her classes to teach the speed reading.

She opened the first speed reading school named *Evelyn Wood's Reading Dynamics*.

Today, this school is present at 61 university and can be proud of 300.000 students that attended the courses over the years.

As you can see, speed reading schools have been around for quite a while and they have certain tradition.

As a reader, you maybe aren't familiar with the fact that every one of us has different ability of receiving and processing new information. Some people learn the fastest when listening to school teachers, participating in a seminar or consulting with an expert from the field. For other people, the easiest way to collect information is from reading materials. Almost everyone has a more or less advanced learning system.

You can consider attending a speed reading school if you want to further improve the way in which you practice speed reading.

I'll mention a few pros and cons of attending these courses. I hope it will give you a bigger picture and make it easier for you to decide if attending these seminars is a good idea.

PROS

1. Speed reading courses usually summarize the most important information. Participants often save time

by learning only the most necessary techniques and methods of speed reading.
2. The participants often receive additional materials in the form of papers and advices about exercises they have to do at home.
3. Foreign language schools often implement the latest discoveries in the field and can provide additional useful information.
4. Experience. Some of the schools had several thousand students so far. The right exercises to be recommended to participants become more apparent over time.
5. Opportunity to meet new people with similar interest and to exchange experiences with them.

CONS

1. Course price. Speed reading courses are often very expensive, which has a negative effect on the number of participants.
2. Lectures usually focus just on one speed reading technique. Books and professional literature sometimes explain up to 10 different techniques, so course presents the readers with fewer choices. It is known for a fact that certain techniques are more easily accepted than others. Schools insisting on certain techniques may become source of frustration for some participants that progress very slowly.
3. Narrow and superficial knowledge. Lack of knowledge on theory and functioning of speed reading which can significantly slow down progress of participants. Teachers often don't have enough

time to focus on all aspects of speed reading techniques.
4. Quality of teachers and applied methods significantly varies. Some schools have just recently been opened and therefore lack teaching experience. The same applies to new teachers.

A curious thing that I noticed while attending the speed reading courses is that most of the participants were female. The course I attended had about 90% female participants. Here's a structure of participants of speed reading courses:

– 50% students
– 30% professionals
– 20% minors.

All things considered, speed reading courses can be a good choice if you wish to further improve yourself in this field. Consider the pros and cons for yourself and choose the type of learning that best suits your needs and capacities.

Test your reading speed!

Now is the time to test your current reading speed. :)
Try to read at your normal speed. Do not read slower or faster than you usually do. This is very important because in that way you'll get a realistic information about your current speed and you will be able to track your progress more accurately in the future.

The following text has been downloaded from Wikipedia and has exactly 1161 words. Link to the original text can be found at the end of the book in the Literature section.

Start the stopwatch from the word "Start" and begin reading.

START

Speed reading is any of the several techniques used to improve one's ability to read quickly, while retaining appropriate level of comprehension. It resembles and is very similar to the less systematic skimming.

Speed Reading Ability

In order to measure the reading speed of a person, we have to test two skills. An actual reading speed of a reader, on one hand, and the level of comprehension of the text. Level of comprehension should not drop with increase of reading speed. In practice, this mostly depends on the ability the tested reader already has, as well as on its previous reading experience. Study carried out by Ronald P. Carvers showed that the drop in the level of comprehension was observed only after an individual exceeded the highest possible reading speed. Practice and previous experience shows that a reader who learns and applies speed reading techniques can improve his reading speed by 2-3 times.

While in the beginning there were different opinions about whether speed reading was a skill that can be practiced, today, this discipline became a generally accepted idea due to the huge success of the existing techniques. A reader who masters the speed reading techniques can achieve reading speed of 800 to 1500 words per minute, while keeping the level of comprehension the same or slightly reduced. Reading speed of an average reader, who does not apply speed reading techniques, can vary around 250 words per minute. The fastest readers in the world are those who spent a long time practicing these techniques and they were capable of reading at a speed of 4000 words per minute. World Record holder in speed reading is Anne Jones. He managed to read the book "Harry Potter and the Deathly Hollows" in just 47 minutes, which means she read at a speed of 4251 words per minute.

Several very interesting facts have been observed in the history of speed reading. In 1969 Mr. Harry McLaughlin studied a group of speed readers and discovered one among them, who he called "Miss L". This person was able to read at a speed up to 9000 words per minute or at an average speed of 3750 words per minute. Some persons are capable of achieving such speeds, although they might seem unattainable at a time. There are other studies that claim there are people capable of reading even faster (Schale 1970: several participants with more than 20.000 words per minute, one person with 41.000 words per minute), however authenticity of this studies is questionable and the test have not been fully verified.

Reading Process

When reading a text, a trained reader will, even if he has no knowledge of speed reading techniques, spend less time looking at individual letters, and will concentrate more on words and phrases the brain recognizes without the need to read individual words. The length of chunks that the brain is capable of receiving and processing is individual and differs depending on a person, text composition and difficulty. In practice, during reading an eye will be strictly focused on small number of letters shown. The main criteria used to follow a text is recognition of words and/or groups of words. These groups of words can be tracked as blocks, which may be interpreted by the reader in the similar way he interprets images that already have meaning stored in the brain. The precondition is that brain is familiar with the groups of words or individual words. If the brain is capable of rearranging the symbolic context provided by the words, then the reading speed can be significantly improved. The ability to process whole words depends on the individual abilities of the reader, composition of the text and external conditions in which reading takes place.

Texts written in Serif font can potentially be read faster and the use of punctuation also improves the possibility of achieving high reading speed. It can also be useful if a text is written in narrow columns. Research showed that narrow bodies of text are easier to read than the wide ones. The reason for this partially lies in the way our eyes operate. For example, in case of a narrow text, an eye does not have to jump from the beginning to the end of the line but can see the entire line instead. This is particularly useful for saving time, because it allows speed readers to significantly improve reading speed by reading several lines at once.

There are currently different theories about how our brain functions and the science does not have a definite explanation about how information is received. There are two ways of receiving information: serial and parallel. Serial reception of information means reading row by row, while parallel means that two or more rows are read simultaneously.

Scientific Studies

Interest in speed reading suddenly increased in 1950s, when the first articles about speed reading started appearing. Evelyn Wood, who has by now opened 61 school of speed reading, thinks that the increase of reading speed from 250 to 1000 words per minute is attainable. She emphasizes the importance of learning and using the speed reading techniques. During her research, Evelyn had the opportunity to meet natural speed readers. These persons were capable of achieving very high reading speeds even without implementing any speed reading techniques. On the other hand, especially during 1960s there were several scientists who raised their suspicion about this technique.

A meta-analysis of speed reading carried out by Musch and Rösler in 2011, which focused on the reading speeds achieved, discusses the huge methodological errors of previous studies. The authors claim that popular literature on this subject is not based on scientific facts and does not give any hard evidence about effectiveness of these techniques.

In general, there is currently a common opinion in scientific literature that there are groups of fast readers, as well as individuals with of the ability of extremely fast reading. On the other hand, the question remains about the extent in which these characteristics can be improved by learning the speed reading techniques.

In 2015 Stiftung Warentest organization conducted comparative tests to examine efficiency of speed reading techniques. The results showed that several respondents increased their reading speed by 50%, while the level of comprehension dropped only slightly.

Criticism Regarding the Speed Reading Techniques

The people who criticize the technique assume that speed readers collect less information than a person who reads at an average speed, i.e. speed below 300 words per minute. At first, this assumption seems provable, however various speed reading studies failed to confirm or dismiss it. A study carried out by B.L. Brown in 1981, which was explicitly focused on reading skills, compared the reading speeds of fast readers and regular readers. Both groups of respondents achieved comprehension level of 65%, while speed readers managed to read 5 to 6 times faster. The assumption that comprehension drops at higher reading speeds was not proved by any scientifically sustainable study so far.

THE END

Here is how you can calculate your average reading speed: Divide the number of words in this text (1161) with the time you took to read it measured in seconds, then multiply the result by 60.

You will get the number of words you can read in a minute.

Write this result at the end of the book in your progress chart.

How to quickly measure your current reading speed

You can test you reading speed by applying a more practical method that lasts just 6 seconds :).
1. Set the timer to 6 seconds.
2. Wait for the timer to go off.
3. Count the number of words you have read.
4. Add a zero to the number and that is your current reading speed per minute.

Conditions You Need to Practice Speed Reading

Influence of work environment on concentration and speed reading

One of the things that are usually overlooked, but which can significantly influence your reading speed is your immediate environment. Take a moment to think about how you feel when you sit at your work desk? Is the feeling positive or negative?

If you feel anxious and can't wait to leave the desk, then you definitely need to make some changes. Below, you will find several tips that can help you create better conditions for comfortable and efficient reading.

1.
Check if your work desk is neat and clear of any needless objects. A book, a desk lamp and a clock are all that you need. All other things will distract you and cause loss of concentration. Phone is particularly not recommended. It is recommended to keep your phone on silent mode when reading, so that no one disturbs you while you work.

2.
Check if you feel comfortable sitting at your work desk. Is the chair too soft or wobbly? Is the desk wide enough? Is the desktop clear? These are small things which can significantly affect the way you feel while sitting at the desk.

If necessary, you can rearrange furniture in your room, buy a new desk or chair. Sell the old one. Everything should come second to you feeling comfortable and relaxed when sitting at the desk.

3.
In order to work more efficiently and improve your speed reading techniques it is recommended to find a quiet and comfortable place without any noise. Too much noise or other distractions can slow down your progress and very quickly lead to you being dissatisfied with the results achieved. I have two advices that can help you find a quiet time of day for reading. If you can, try getting up early. Preferably one hour before other members of your household. This is great time of day, because it is absolutely quiet, so you can fully devote yourself to reading. The second advice is regarding public libraries. These institutions are often used by students that prepare for the exams. Visit several public libraries that are close to you and see if this environment suits you better. Being surrounded by large number of people who read, prepare exams and professionally develop themselves can give you additional boost, that will motivate you to try even harder. The atmosphere in the libraries can also help you concentrate and gain new knowledge more easily.

Sometimes a man can feel lonely if he spends long periods of time reading and not leaving his home, so this is a good idea, since it will help you meet and socialize with new friends.

Correct sitting posture

4.
Well-lit and ventilated work space is a precondition for speed reading. Make sure that your desk is as close to a window as it can be. Daylight is always a better choice than artificial light. Reading under a bad light can after sometime cause deterioration of vision. If you are a night reader, make sure that a lamp is positioned in such way that it does not bother your eyes and that light bulb is of proper power. Also, the importance of well-ventilated room is often neglected nowadays. People, especially during winter, tend to open windows and ventilate rooms less frequently. If you are reading in too hot and stifling room, instead of being focused on reading, you are more likely to fall asleep. Remember to open a window at least once a day for 15

minutes and let the fresh air into the room. A colder room will help you achieve higher levels of concentration.

In short, an ideal reading spot has to meet the following requirements and be:
– neat and clean;
– comfortable;
– quiet;
– well lit;
– well ventilated.

What time of day is the best for reading?

Our concentration is known to vary during a day. Sometimes we are best concentrated in the morning, while sometimes we feel concentrated in the afternoon or in the evening. Have you ever had a chance to explore during what time of day you have the best attention and memory? If you are a student, then you probably know the time of day during which your studying is the most effective. People have different habits and therefore their concentration and focus are at the highest level during different times of day. Most people usually feel the best concentrated in the morning. Night studying is also very common. Speaking from my personal experience, I am the most energized and concentrated in the morning, between 6 and 10 a.m.

Learning and practicing of speed reading techniques requires a large amount of attention and focus. It is not easy to change your reading habits and quickly learn all the new information. Make your learning experience easier by discovering a time of day during which you are the most efficient. If you are feeling tired or your mind is wondering take a walk in fresh air, play some sports, and continue reading after that. However, try to choose a time of day during which you will be focused on reading only.

Our habits often affect the quality of our life. This is why the activities we repeat every day are so important. Did you know that recent studies show that every day we repeat about 90% of the activities we did the day before? So, make a summary of the good and bad habits you express during a day. Let's say that you spend one hour a day watching television and one hour a day on social media or the Internet. It is 60 hours a month. In 60 hours an average person can read about 2000 pages of text. A speed reader can read 4000 to 10000 pages during the same period. Let's say for example that an average book has about 300 pages. That is 6 new books if you are an average, slow reader or up to 33 new books if you learned the speed reading techniques. Just imagine how your life would change if you had a habit of reading this many books every month. Regardless whether it is a professional literature, fiction or classic literature, you would very quickly notice huge positive changes in both your private and professional life.

I am often asked: what is the best place for reading? Some people read in bed, tram or similar locations. In my opinion, whether you study or practice, the best place to read is certainly your work desk. That's where you will be able to concentrate and focus the most. If, however, you read to relax and for fun, a bed or an armchair is also a good choice.

Food with positive effect on concentration

The food we consume during the day greatly influences our level of concentration, energy, as well as our ability of doing daily tasks with ease. As the time passes, tasks are piling up, while energy and concentration are drained. The question is what we can do to raise the levels of energy and mood during the day which are required to fulfil our plans. One of the best advices is to change or improve our eating habits.

It is a well-known fact that certain food positively affects our concentration and memory. On the other hand, some types of food have negative effect on these abilities.

In this chapter I will try to make a list of food that can help you study, achieve higher level of focus and more easily complete your everyday tasks.

GOOD FOOD

Foods which contains vitamin E, C and B, pectin, enzymes, magnesium and calcium are well-known for its effect on concentration, brain activity and memory.

LEGUMES

The following legumes are rich with vitamin E, which is important for our intellectual activities:
— walnut
— almond
— peanuts

– oat
– hazelnut
– sunflower, sesame and flax seed.

A handful of this food is enough for one day.

FRUIT

Fruit and vegetable rich diet has positive effects on memory, concentration and motor coordination.

Blueberries and avocado are especially useful for good memory and concentration. You'll have no problem finding blueberry juice in the market near you. Just remember to check the percentage of fruit in the juice. You should choose the juices with the highest level of fruit.

All citruses are recommended and you should definitely include them in your daily diet. The best citruses are: oranges, tangerines, lemon, pomelo and grapefruit.

In the winter time, when fresh fruit is hard to find, just buy dried fruit. Just beware of overeating. Dried fruit has three times more calories than the fresh one.

Pomegranate is also highly recommended as a dietary supplement.

OMEGA 3 FATTY ACIDS

Omega 3 fatty acids (DHA) make up 25% of our brain. Our body is not capable of synthetizing this substance, so it can only be obtained from food. Fat sea fish, such as salmon, mackerel, sardine, tuna have the highest percentage of these acids.

It is recommended that at least twice a week your main meal should contain one of the abovementioned types of fish.

COFFEE
Coffee has its positive and negative aspects. In my case, it is more harmful than useful. However, the effects and reaction of the body differ from person to person. If you notice that after drinking coffee you feel energized and find it easier to concentrate, than feel free to make this drink a part of your daily routine.

TEAS
It is a well-known fact that there are certain teas which raise the level of concentration. Tea itself usually contains caffeine. Unlike coffee, our body gradually absorbs this substance over a long time period. In this way brain activity is gradually improved and there are no sudden pikes and drops.

Teas that increase concentration are:
– black tea (has high level of caffeine)
– ginger, ginseng and ginkgo biloba tea
– rosemary tea (improves memory)
– peach and quince tea
– apple tea
– blueberry tea.

You can also try out green tea and mint tea.

VEGETABLES

Green and fresh vegetables have positive effect on the entire body, not only on our ability to concentrate and focus. Pay particular attention to:
– kale
– spinach
– parsley
– broccoli.

These vegetables are high on vitamin K which improves brain functions and restores memory. The following food also has beneficial effect on our brain:
– soya
– peas
– lentils
– carrots.

Find out what is your favourite vegetable yourself, and then create a weekly menu that suits you.

SWEETS

There are very few sweets that have positive effect on our brain and ability to concentrate. Most of them have negative effect.

However, there are two foods that you should certainly consider if you have trouble with concentration and bad memory. Dark chocolate and honey. Dark chocolate, unlike the regular chocolate, has several times higher content of cocoa, which positively affects concentration.

Natural honey has favourable effect on the entire body, not only on concentration. You should still be careful, since commercial honey is sometimes overheated several times, so it loses most of its beneficial characteristics. It's better to buy honey directly from beekeepers. It often has higher level of minerals than the industrial-made honey from the store. The darker honey is, the better.

OIL
Cold pressed oils, such as olive oil, coconut oil and sesame oil are a much better choice than the hot pressed oils. It is a proven fact that olive oil improves thinking, memory and balances our mood.

QUINOA
Quinoa seed originates from South America, from the Andean Region, and does not contain gluten. Besides containing high level of proteins, fibres, vitamin B and iron, it also contains all eight amino acids.

The following foods can also have positive effects on our ability to concentrate, our attention and focus: chicken, Greek yogurt, eggs, beet juice.

BAD FOOD

The following foods very often have bad effect on our ability to concentrate and study, so they should be avoided. I'll list them by harmfulness:
– sweets and sweetened drinks
– milk (can slow down metabolism)
– white bread
– food made from refined flour and sugar
– food made from refined carbohydrates.

In general, try to avoid having large meals. An interesting study showed that lifespan of laboratory animals that received 30-50% less calories was 33 to 50% longer.

Food that rejuvenates the brain

Neurons we have are provided to us at the very beginning of our life and as the time passes, there are fewer and fewer of them. Depending on our diet, this process can be slowed down. In his book "Secrets of Cleansing Your Brain", Georgij Nazarov suggests several useful foods that have positive effect on and rejuvenate our brain.

Natural calcium from egg shells
– Tip of the knife or a teaspoon

Pollen powder
– Two or more teaspoons

Royal jelly
– According to individual needs

Vitamin C – 500 mg or more
Vitamin E – 100 mg or more
Omega 3 from fish oil – 1.000 mg or more
Beer yeast – two teaspoons
Apple cider vinegar – two teaspoons
Green tea – two cups or more
Freshly squeezed juices – half a litre or more
Garlic – as much as possible
Ginger – quarter of teaspoon
Algae – two teaspoons or more
Linseed oil – two teaspoons a day
Sprouted grains and legumes – two tablespoons
Cinnamon – tip of a knife, with a meal

INTERESTING FACTS

It is interesting how essential oils and scents affect our concentration and attention. A study has been conducted on people who professionally play games. During a break, one group was given mint and rosemary to smell. After the break, this group showed much better results compared to other players.

Another study showed that a slice of freshly cut lemon kept in your work space can increase concentration up to 50%. You can try and rub fresh mint on your hands and leave it in your study room. A smell of mint in a study room can increase concentration up to 40%. These two substances also significantly affect the vigilance, which has been confirmed by several studies.

Having breakfast at the same time every day improved memory and concentration of school children both during classes and after school. For this reason you should try not to skip breakfast. Make sure that it mostly consists of fresh foods, rich with natural sugars, that will help you wake up faster.

Our brain represents only 2% of our body mass, but it spends up to 20% of oxygen. Therefore, you should make sure to spend at least half an hour a day on fresh air. The best results are achieved if you do this before studying. Or maybe between tasks. Better ventilated room and breaks on fresh air will help you focus and concentrate on your daily tasks.

Most of our body consists of liquid. Our brain is made of 75% water. Recommended intake of fluid during a day is 2 - 3 litres. A man takes about half a litre of daily fluid requirements through food. So, you should drink about 1,5 to 2,5 litres of water depending on your weight and daily activities.
Higher intake of fluids will help you feel more vigilant and energized.

SUMMARY

The following conditions are required for quality and efficient studying and concentration.

1. Make sure that your diet provides you the highest possible energy during the day and makes you feel healthy. So, you should eat: fresh fruit and vegetables, fish, legumes, tea, honey and dark chocolate.

2. Avoid sweets and sweetened drinks, white bread and refined food.

3. Take a time to exercise a little every day. Preferably in fresh air. Always stay in a well-ventilated room. Don't skip breakfast and get enough sleep.

Influence of a healthy lifestyle on reading speed

The speed by which you improve when learning the advanced speed reading techniques largely depends on your lifestyle. If you are not physically active, you eat unhealthily or work hard all day, you will not have enough time and energy to properly devote yourself to speed reading exercises.

Make a smarter plan of your day and organize your time in a better and more productive way. Here's my suggested morning routine:
– wake up at 5.00 a.m.
– read a book of choice in bed until 5.45 a.m.
– get up and perform stretching exercises until 6.00 a.m.
– learn and improve yourself in the field that is your current top priority until 6.45 a.m.
– go for a 30-minute run or walk while listening a book from *Audible* service
–your morning routine should be over by 7.15 a.m. and you will be ready for a new day.

If you use this routine every day, you will see constant improvement of your skills and in the number of books read in a month.

Eye Exercises and How to Preserve Your Vision

Did you know that 50% of students from Great Britain have some sort of vision problem, and that more that 80% of population of Singapore suffers from near-sightedness? In Australia this percentage is just 10%.

Vision problems are usually caused by looking at close objects over long periods of time, as it is the case with reading or looking at your phone. Our eyes are not intended just for looking at near objects. It is very important to use our vision for looking at distant objects.

In Australia students spend up to three hours a day outdoors. This is one of the most important reasons why only 7% of children suffer from near-sightedness.

Your goal of learning the speed reading techniques should not be at the expense of your sight. Make regular breaks and try to look at distant objects whenever you have time. Focus changing and exercising of peripheral vision can also be of help. Preferably, you should often change focus and look at objects at different distance. In this way you can practice your sight and significantly reduce the possibility of near-sightedness. There is a book by Viktor Medvedev that I would kindly recommend: *Seeing Without Glasses.* The author made an exceptional effort and gave detailed description of the way in which our eyes function and explained a lot of exercises for preserving vision.

Speaking from personal experience, thanks to the advices from this book I stopped further increase of my dioptre. My dioptres used to increase each year, until I read this book and started doing a few simple everyday exercises.

If you frequently use a computer, I recommend you to install an application named *eyeCare*. This program reminds you every 20 minutes to look at a distant object for 20 seconds. World Health Organization has officially recognized the benefits of this method for preservation of sight.

Theoretical Part

Bad Reading Habits

Did you know that an average adult doesn't read faster than a seventh-grader? The reading technique is fully developed by then and it stops improving later in life. It is a very common case that even people with university degrees don't improve their reading speed during education. Most people have never come across the term "speed reading" and are not familiar with this subject. You will very soon notice the advantages you gained from reading this book in your everyday life.

There are a few basic things about reading that we do wrong. Look at the examples below and try to remember them.

Bad habit no. 1 – reading individual words

The picture below shows how an average reader reads a text. You will notice how his eyes "jump" from one word to another.

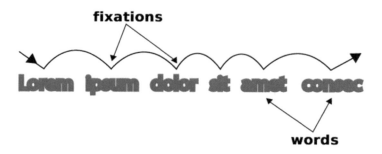

This reading method is very slow, for the obvious reasons. In this example we place our eyes on each word, stop and then go to the next word. In practice, this takes a lot of time and is unnecessary.

Human eye is capable of seeing several words at once. Trained readers often read four or more lines at a time, thus not losing time on reading individual words. In that way they are capable of achieving high reading speeds by using the ability of reading with peripheral vision, which is something everyone can do.

Here's a quick math. Let' say, for example, that one line of text has 15 words, which in practice means that if you use this method you will have 15 fixations on 15 individual words in a single line. On the other hand, a trained reader can read this line with only three to four fixations.

Over the years your brain and sight get used to reading individual words. This book aims to reprogram the way you look at the text and receive information. When you start practicing it is possible that you will have problems with comprehension, but don't worry about that. In time, as you practice, your comprehension level will improve.

Let's now see how a trained reader reads this text.

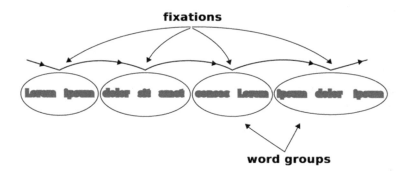

You will notice that there is as much as three times less fixations. This is an example of correct reading, where a reader looks at several words at a time. In the beginning this can mean two to three words, but in time, as you practice, this number will increase. Some of the best readers in the world have perfected their vision so much that they are capable of reading an entire line with just one look. For the beginning, you should be satisfied if you develop a habit of reading more than one word at a time.

So, from now on, try reading the material from a wider perspective and set your sight on several words at once. As for comprehension, while you practice it is sufficient to keep comprehension level at 50%. This percentage will improve as you practice.

Bad habit no. 2 – internally repeating the words you read

Subvocalization or internal repetition of words read is a

very common practice. This habit is very widespread and originates from a very early age and the time when a person learns how to read. Internal repetition of words was necessary at the time to be able to understand the text. The problem is when adult readers continue to use this habit. Why is this such a bad habit? This is a bad habit because the speed at which we are internally repeating words is far slower than our ability to see and read the text. Therefore, this habit has a negative effect on our reading speed. Some of the advocates of speed reading state that subvocalization must be completely eliminated, however, I think that it has to be reduced to the minimum level. So, from now on, try to read without the words you read echoing in your head. Try to capture the ideas and thoughts of the author with your sight.

Speed reading techniques are based on the reading technique called *Brain Reading.* Our brain is capable of processing a huge amount of text, far more than we are capable of pronouncing.

Let me now give you an example that shows that subvocalization is unnecessary. Look at the traffic signs, for example. When you see them, you do not have to internally repeat the meaning of each sign in order to understand it. If you see a sign for pedestrian crossing, you simply know what it means. You do not have to internally repeat "pedestrian crossing" in order to understand the meaning.

Bad habit no. 3 – back-skipping

Everyone has been in the situation of reading a text for 15 or more minutes, but not knowing afterwards what he has just read. Such drop in concentration is the main cause of extremely slow reading. This usually happens when a text is not interesting to the reader. Then we start thinking about other unrelated things. That is when the reading suffers the most and we are uncapable of accomplishing the goal of reading a book. Besides a huge waste of time, this could also cause negative emotions due to slow progress. This problem can easily be overcome with faster reading. Just remember the example about carrying a bag of cement from one place to another.

The picture below shows the eye movement of an unfocused reader:

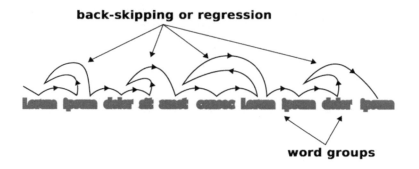

You can see a large number of fixations.
In practice, the reader does read the text, but he continues back-skipping to what has already been read in an attempt to improve comprehension. Often, he returns to reread entire paragraphs. It's pretty obvious why such reading should be avoided at all costs. Just count the number of fixations in this case. A total of 16 fixations on just 10 words. If you take into account all the previous paragraphs, the number grows. This is the slowest and the least efficient type of reading.

In the rest of the book and in the future, when you read other materials, try to avoid back-skipping. In case you didn't fully comprehend something you would usually find explanations later in the text.

A speed reader would focus on reading new content, as fast as possible and with the highest level of comprehension. Try to always look at the reading process from this perspective and don't lose time on regression.

CHAPTER SUMMARY

Try to avoid whenever possible:
– reading individual words
– internally repeating words (subvocalization)
– back-skipping to the already read text

Technique of Speed Reading with Visual Aid

During its evolution the human eye developed the ability to more quickly notice and track moving objects. You probably know that for several thousand years before the modern age humans lived as hunters, meaning that the slightest move in the environment often meant the difference between spotting a predator or not. This is the reason why our eyes have over time acquired the ability to more easily notice and follow movement. Knowing this, we can assume that book reading is not a natural, evolutional activity for the eye. The main reason behind many eye disorders and vision deterioration is usually the fact that over a long period of time we only use one segment of our vision. Therefore, people who work a lot on computer or read a lot, often have problems with seeing at larger distances. This is the result of spending more time looking at nearby objects and less time looking at distant objects. It's the same as with any other skill. What we don't use becomes less developed over time. Speaking of that, I just remembered an interesting saying I read recently. A man who does not improve is in regression. There is no middle value between these two extremes. But, let's get back to the subject. In order for an eye to function normally, it is necessary that we often change focus. By that I mean looking at objects located at different distances and in different parts of our field of vision.

Let's see how this information can be applied to speed reading techniques. The picture below shows a hand holding a guide which traces a line of text.

Um die Fähigkeit des Schnelllesens einer Person messen zu können, müssen die Faktoren der Lesegeschwindigkeit und des Textverständnisses gleichzeitig überprüft werden: Unter einer hohen Lesegeschwindigkeit darf die Lesekompetenz nicht leiden. Tatsächlich hängt dieses aber von der Lesekompetenz ab: Überschreitet ein Leser eine gewisse Lesegeschwindigkeit, wird Untersuchungen Ronald P. Carvers zufolge seine Lesekompetenz in ungefähr antiproportionalem Verhältnis abnehmen.

Während es zunächst als umstritten galt, ob schnelles Lesen trainiert werden kann, wird dieser Umstand in der Wissenschaft auch aufgrund diverser offensichtlich erfolgreicher Techniken zum Schnelllesen weitgehend akzeptiert. Mit den erlernbaren Techniken des Schnelllesens sind für geübte Leser Werte von 800 bis 1.500 gelesenen Wörtern pro Minute erreichbar, ohne das Textverständnis erheblich einzuschränken. Bei einem durchschnittlichen geübten Leser, der allerdings keine Techniken des Schnelllesens verwendet, wird von einem durchschnittlichen Wert von etwa 250 Wörtern pro Minute ausgegangen. Von einigen Schnelllesern wurden auch über längere Zeiträume wesentlich höhere Werte von über 4.000 Wörtern pro Minute erreicht. Den Weltrekord im Schnelllesen soll dabei Anne Jones halten, die das Buch Harry Potter und die Heiligtümer des Todes in einer Zeit von 47 Minuten gelesen haben soll, was einen Lesewert von 4.251 Wörtern pro Minute ergibt.

Bereits 1969 untersuchte G. Har

Since we know that it is easier for an eye to follow a moving object, by using the guide you make it easier for your eye to read. From now on, whenever you read a text, use a guide as shown in the picture.

The reading with the help of a visual aid will make it easier for your eye to focus on the line, thus allowing even higher reading speed. According to my research, that would lead to 20 to 30% faster reading to begin with. Everything you need is a pencil or any other object similar to a stick. You can use a painting brush, knitting needle, chopsticks or a similar object. Ideally, you should use a small wooden stick which is two to three times thinner than a chopstick. The tip should be pointed on one side.

In the remaining part of the book, start tracing every line that you read. From time to time increase the speed by which you trace the lines. Even after just 5-15 minutes of practice you will notice that your reading speed has significantly improved.

When reading, don't forget to look at three or more words at a time. In that way you also improve your peripheral vision, thus additionally increasing your reading speed.

Some trained readers are capable of using this method by tracing two lines at the same time. In practice this means that this technique alone allows for doubled reading speed. However, it takes a lot of time to master this technique. For now, you should just focus on a single line and follow the above instructions. You should use a visual aid from now on whenever you are reading.

Tips to Improve Comprehension Level

Most students and people who read a lot, have a problem of comprehending the text from time to time. Sometimes the reason lies in the lack of interest in the matter, but sometimes a text can be unclear. In these situations, our studying and reading efficiency often become very low. In general, the time passes, our mind wonders, and a reader receives only a small portion of information. The goal of this chapter is to prevent these situations from happening. There are several practical tips that helped me, that I hope will help you too. The main goal of this chapter is therefore to achieve the highest level of concentration and the best possible level of comprehension.

Tip no. 1
Select a specific time or part of day that you will devote just to reading. Try to always start and end reading at the same time. In this way you'll develop a habit which will make reading and learning significantly easier.

Tip no. 2
Set your goals before you start reading. Ask yourself the following questions:

What do I want to accomplish by reading this text?
How much time I can spend on reading?
Which part/chapter I plan to read today?

Try to keep your goals realistic and clear. An unrealistic goal can discourage you and cause you to give up.

It is better to split big and hard goals into several smaller ones. For example, you can say that writing a 500-page book is a difficult task. However, if you write just five pages a day it will take you three months to finish the job.

Tip no. 3
Always read at the same place. Avoid reading in bed or in armchair. The best focus is achieved when reading at your work desk.

Tip no. 4
Before you start reading, quickly go through the text. First read just the chapter titles, names of sections, graphs, bold text. Try to create a quick summary of the material you are about to read. Take a few minutes for this activity every time before you start reading.

This tip will allow you to create a general overview of the text you read and help you improve the level of comprehension.

Tip no. 5
Ask yourself questions about the text you have just read. The best results are achieved if you answer questions after you read a chapter or after 20 minutes of reading. This tip will help you extract the most important information from the text.

Here are some questions you can ask yourself:

What is the text I have read about?
What characters are mentioned in the text?

What facts are especially important to understand the text? What is the main idea the author wants to convey to the reader of this section?

You can make the questions yourself, depending on the type of texts you read. The goal is to create several logical segments and divide the text in a way that makes it clearer.

Tip no. 6
Motivation. A lot of books are written about motivation, so I will not talk a lot on this subject.

Each and every one of us has certain goals and wishes he wants to accomplish. Ask yourself if reading of certain text gets you closer to the goals you have set. If no, it's better to leave the book you are reading and find the one that suits you better.

A number of readers successfully applies the method of autosuggestion to advance more easily. Find out what has the best effect on you and try to adhere to your daily plans and tasks.

Below you will find several quotes on motivation. If you find it especially hard to continue working, just read the next page.

A few of the most beautiful quotes on motivation

"You take your life in your own hands, and what happens? A terrible thing: no one to blame."
Erica Jong

"The two most important days in your life are the day you are born and the day you find out why."
Mark Twain

"Whether you think you can, or you think you can't--you're right."
Henry Ford

"There is only one way to avoid criticism: do nothing, say nothing, and be nothing."
Aristotle

"Remember that sometimes not getting what you want is a wonderful stroke of luck."
Dalai Lama

"Instead of wondering when your next vacation is, maybe you should set up a life you don't need to escape from."
Seth Godin

"I am not a product of my circumstances. I am a product of my decisions."
Stephen Covey

"The best way to predict your future is to create it."

Abraham Lincoln

"Look at a day when you are supremely satisfied at the end. It's not a day when you lounge around doing nothing; it's a day you've had everything to do and you've done it."
Margaret Thatcher

"You can't cut down every tree with the first chop."
Chinese proverb

"If I must fall, may it be from a high place. "
Paulo Coelho

"Just do the best you can. No one can do more than that."
John Wooden

"There is no man living who isn't capable of doing more than he thinks he can do."
Henry Ford

"Everything is achievable! Impossible is a word to be found only in the dictionary of fools. "
Napoleon I Bonaparte

Causes of Bad Concentration and Comprehension

There are several causes that negatively affect our comprehension level. In the following chapter we'll mention just a few. After every cause, I will give an advice on how to overcome it.

1. Small vocabulary

One of the biggest obstacles you can face is that you are not familiar with the terminology (expert terms) used in a book. It is very common in case for expert literature, where in the beginning you have to use a dictionary from time to time.

Solution:
You can solve this problem by active reading and persistence. Over time your vocabulary will grow with every new book you read and you will not have to stop while reading a text.

2. Difficulty of the reading material

There are texts of various difficulty and length. It is not the same to read a new novel of your favourite author or human anatomy book with many Latin terms.

Solution:
Adjust your reading speed. Sometimes you have to reduce the reading speed in order to successfully comprehend the material. This is a common case when you are reading a complex book for the first time. With every new read this problem will become less prominent until it finally

disappears. We often can't fully comprehend complex text after one reading. After rereading a chapter or paragraph you will have a much better insight into the idea of the text.

3. Insufficient focus, bad organization and lack of motivation

Text comprehension and our reading speed are mostly determined by our ability to focus on the text. Also, bad organization and lack of motivation can significantly affect our reading performance.

Solution:
Apply the six advices mentioned a few pages earlier.

Test you level of comprehension!

Below you will find an example of a text which you can use to test your current level of comprehension.

After the text, you will find 10 questions that you have to answer, so read carefully. Don't get discouraged if your score is low. The goal of the book is that you gradually increase your level of comprehension, so don't be too much bothered by the score. Just remember that every year the total knowledge available to man increases by 30%.

Another fun fact: According to statistics, two million scientific papers are published around the globe every year. Less than 1% of this number was being published one hundred years ago (in Einstein's time).

Therefore, we are unable to remember and process all the information for practical reasons. The main goal we have to pursue is to improve the ability to separate important from unimportant while reading, thus achieving higher level of comprehension.

Let's begin! Start a stopwatch and begin reading.

Penguins

Penguins are a group of aquatic, flightless birds, that live almost exclusively in the Southern Hemisphere. They include six subfamilies with 17 or 20 species, depending on the author. Penguins are adapted to aquatic life with wings that have evolved to flippers. They have black backs and wings with white fronts. Penguins feed on krill, fish, squid and other forms of sea life caught while swimming underwater. They spend about half of their lives in the oceans.

Although almost all penguin species are native to the Southern Hemisphere, they are not found only in cold climate, such as Antarctica. In fact, only a few species of penguin live so far south. Several species are found in the temperate zone, and one species, the Galapagos penguin, lives near the equator.

The largest living species is the emperor penguin; on average, adults are about 1.1m tall and weigh 35 kg. The smallest penguin species is the little blue penguin, which stands around 40 cm tall and weighs 1 kg. Larger penguins inhabit colder regions, while smaller penguins are generally found in temperate or even tropical climates. Some prehistoric species attained enormous sizes, becoming as tall or as heavy as an adult human.

Penguins are superbly adapted to aquatic life. Their vestigial wings have become flippers, useless for flight. In the water, however, penguins are astonishingly agile. Within the smooth plumage a layer of air is preserved, ensuring buoyancy. Most of the species weigh just slightly more than water their body exerts, which allows them to dive with ease. Diving penguins reach 5 to 10 km/h, though some species reach up to 36 km/h. They can stay underwater up to 20 minutes. When swimming fast, they paddle with their wings. Actually, they use their webbed feet as rudders, while propelling themselves by wings. When swimming slowly they use only their feet.

When on land, penguins primarily use their short and stiff tails, as well as their wings to maintain balance for their upright stance. Since their legs are set far back on the body, they can only maintain an upright posture. On land penguins either waddle or slide on their bellies.

Depending on the species, penguins can grow from 40 cm to 120 cm in height. The tallest penguin species is the emperor penguin, which stands around 1.1 m tall and weighs more than 35 kg. The smallest penguin species is the little blue penguin, which stands around 43 cm and weighs 1 kg. Larger penguins usually inhabit colder regions, while smaller penguins are generally found in temperate or even tropical climates, which is in accordance with Bergmann's rule.

Some prehistoric species attained enormous sizes, becoming as tall or as heavy as an adult human. These were not restricted to Antarctic regions, but vast Subantarctic region as well. Fossils found in Peru in 2007 provide evidence of penguin species that was about 1.5 m high and had a beak that was 30 cm long, making it the largest penguin in the world. Fossils found in Atacama Desert show they didn't need cold environment to survive. The fossils discovered are about 36.000 years old and date from one of the hottest periods in the last 65 million years.

Penguin eyes are adapted to underwater vision. There is a theory according to which penguins are near-sighted on land, although research has not supported this hypothesis. In deep-diving species, such as emperor penguins, pupils are extremely flexible, which allows their eyes to quickly adjust to different amount of light available at water surface and several hundred meters below the surface. Based on the pigment content it is presumed that penguins are more sensitive of blue, than red wavelengths, as well as that they can see the ultraviolet light as well. Since the red wavelengths are filtered and lost in the top water layers, this feature can be understood as evolutional adaptation to the environment.

As the most birds, penguins don't have an outer ear. When diving, their ears are closed air-tight by feathers. In large penguin species the edge of the outer ear is so enlarged that it can be closed to protect inner and middle ear from damage that can be caused by pressure during deep diving. Penguins' hearing is as good as in any other bird species. (Hearing range from 100 to 15.000 Hz, with the best hearing between 600 and 4000 Hz), which allows them to hear their chicks or partners in large colonies.

On land, penguins communicate with each other by calls that are similar to the sound of a trumpet. There is a species called a "jackass" penguins, known for its donkey-like bray. However, penguins don't make any sounds when they are in water to prevent giving away their position to predators or scaring the possible pray.

Thermal insulation is provided by three-centimetre-thick layer of fat covered with three layers of airtight, closely overlapped and equally distributed feathers. Penguins have no body parts without feathers. The only exception are some tropical species that have bare patches on their faces. The air trapped in layers of feather is another way to efficiently prevent heat loss.

Penguins can control blood flow in their limbs, thus conserving the heat and preventing the limbs from freezing.

In the extreme cold of the Antarctic winter, the females are at sea fishing for food leaving the males to brave the weather by themselves. They often huddle together to keep warm and rotate positions to make sure that each penguin gets a turn in the centre of the heat pack.

On the other hand, some tropical species have overheating problems. In order to prevent that, penguins developed oversized flippers compared to other species, which increases the surface through which blood can be cooled down. Besides that, some species have bare patches on their faces, which allows them to cool down faster in the shades.

Penguins spend half of their lives in water and the other half on land, although according to some sources they spend up to 75% of their lives in water. Some species leave the water only to mate and during moulting. Depending on the species, specimens can live 15 to 20 years or longer.

They feed mostly on krill, fish, squid and other forms of small sea life. Penguins living closer to Antarctica mostly feed on krill, while the northern species mostly feed on fish. Penguins catch prey with their bills and swallow it whole while swimming.

When in water, they satisfy their thirst through water obtained from the prey or by drinking small amounts of sea, salt water, thanks to their supraorbital gland that filters the excess salt from the bloodstream. The salt is excreted in a concentrated fluid from the nasal passages. This adaptation is common for sea creatures, including the aquatic birds, such as penguin. On land they get water from eating small amounts of snow.

Penguins build primitive nests on land. Actually, when you look at the part of Antarctica inhabited by birds, you can notices nesting zones and areas of different bird species. Penguins mostly nest in the zones that are closest to the sea, while other zones are populated by cormorants and skuas. Only six species nest on Antarctica, while others nest near the coast of Africa, Australia and New Zealand, as well as South America. They nest in colonies, which means they gather in big flocks. There can be millions of penguins in a single colony. Nests are often located at some distance from the shore, because penguins do not feed exclusively from the sea, but often take walking tours to the water and back. Gerald Durrell, a researcher, followed a colony of penguins in Patagonia that had almost 2 million individuals and nested at some 3 kilometres from the sea. Parents had to take trips across sandy dunes and were able to unmistakably recognize their nest and chicks, among thousands of hungry younglings begging for food. They recognize each other by sounds, but usually communicate by creaks, clicks and gestures. Some couples nest at the same place every year. Nests are made from pebbles or plants. They are usually made in sheltered locations, such as tunnels (burrows) or cracks in rocks. Nests can also be made in the open. During courtship, males of some species, such as Adélie penguin, offer females pebbles as gifts that can be used to build a nest. Penguins are generally known for their peculiar courtship. Some penguins mate for life, some just for one season. Emperor penguin lays one egg per seasons, while other species lay two eggs, which cared for by both male and female. During strong winters, females spend a few months at sea hunting for food, while males stay on land and sit on eggs. When female returns, they share the responsibilities. It often happens that a female feeds a male individual with partially digested fish, while male emperor penguin, exhausted after two months of starvation, goes to sea to look for food. Chicks with weak thermal regulation are taken care by their mothers only, while other chicks are under supervision of both father and mother. Some species even have a sort of a pouch on their bellies in which they can keep an egg. They keep their feet together and move in small jumps, only if necessary.

Some species, such as emperor penguin, assemble chicks in large groups, so called *crèches*. These groups are organized for better protection and mutual heating. When parents show up with food, they call for their chicks and feed them outside the crèches. Young penguins cannot take care of themselves until they grow up to a certain size and before they grow adult feathers.

As with many other species, penguins show homosexual behaviour. It is interesting that two male penguins usually mate for life. They even create a nest in which they keep a stone as a surrogate egg.

If a penguin, male or female, happens to lose a chick or an egg, he sometimes tries to steal a chick from another individual. Science doesn't have explanation for this behaviour - why would a parent raise and invest into other penguin's offspring, a behaviour which is contrary to the theory of evolution. There are, however, some explanations for this unusual behaviour. Firstly, by raising a chick the kidnapper gains experience, thus increasing the probability of having own chicks in the future. Secondly, due to seemingly successful reproduction, the individual will have more success in finding a partner during the next mating season. And thirdly, a penguin may create a bond with the kidnapped chick, which may prove helpful during the next mating season. However, there is a realistic danger of getting injured by the real parent during the kidnapping attempt, as well as the problem of wasting energy and effort on chick, while not spreading own genes. In a way, it is not certain if such behaviour represents an evolutional advantage or is the result of mistake made by individuals unable to recognize their own chick.

The biggest natural enemies of penguins are sea predators, such as leopard seal, sharks and orca. Leopard seal is a lone, but very efficient penguin hunter that chases them around blocks of ice. When penguins dive into water, the leopard seal usually waits below the iceberg, where penguins can't see it, and when the water starts to foam, the seal starts catching them. If it hunts down one and eats it, the seal usually ends the hunt and other penguins can move freely. It is estimated that about 5% of Adélie penguin are eaten by leopard seals. It is probably due to this and other dangers found in water why penguins rarely decide to jump into water and often wait up to half an hour at the edge of an iceberg or on the shore. When one of them gathers enough courage and jumps in, everyone else soon follows.

If chicks or eggs are left unprotected, they easily become pray to seagulls and skuas. Adult penguins defend from these predators by using their strong beaks.

Penguins, such as southern rockhopper penguin, Adélie and emperor penguin are typical representatives of Australasian realm fauna. According to such zoogeographical division, penguins inhabit Patagonian (or Holantarctic) area. Although all penguin species live in the Southern Hemisphere, in spite of the popular belief that they live in cold area, such as Antarctica, there are actually just a few species that live very far south, while some species even live in hot regions. Larger penguins usually inhabit colder regions, while smaller penguins are generally found in temperate or even tropical climates, which is in accordance with Bergmann's rule.

They can often be found in coastal waters of Antarctica, New Zealand, South Australia, South Africa, on Falkland Islands located by the east coast of South America, but on the west coast as well, all the way to Peru and on Galapagos near the equator (Galapagos penguin). Since penguins are fond of colder areas, they appear in tropical regions only if there are cold sea currents. Penguins use cold currents to migrate, which is one of the reasons they are found in Galapagos. That is the case with Humboldt Current flowing by the west coast of South America (Humboldt penguin), as well as with Bengal Current along the west coast of Africa reaching all the way to equator (jackass penguin).

Most of the species live between 45th and 60th parallel south. Most penguins live near Antarctica or on nearby islands.

True habitat of penguins is the open sea to which they are highly adapted. They live on rocky coasts of southern continents, cold temperate forests, subtropical sandy beaches, on cooled lava with almost no vegetation, on Subantarctic grasslands and Antarctic ice. While tropical species stay in their region, other species migrate even few hundred kilometres to get to the hatching area.

In the 20th century, there are four penguin species that are considered endangered - Galapagos, yellow-eyed penguin, jackass penguin and Fjordland penguin, while Magellanic penguin, Humboldt penguin and several other species are considered vulnerable. In the past, entire penguin colonies were extinct, when they were hunted for fat and eggs , that were used for food, while today penguins face other dangers.

There were several millions of jackass penguins in the previous century, while currently there are just 50.000 and their number continues to drop. It is presumed that the biggest cause of such decrease in numbers is commercial fishing in their habitat, which causes the food shortages.

In New Zealand, which is a habitat of Fjordland and and yellow-eyed penguin, and where human population continues to expand, the predators brought by humans (cats, dogs, rats, etc.) increasingly threaten penguins by attacking them and their eggs. People living in New Zealand continue to expand to nesting and mating areas of penguins, hindering penguins' usual life.

Galapagos penguins are struck by the problems caused by presence of humans and their predators, which caused their population to be limited to only two islands. On the other hand, climate change which caused the "El Ninho" effect, that occasionally causes dramatic drop in quantity of fish, also led to the reduction of population of Galapagos penguins in the 1980s and 1990s. According to the count of "Charles Darwin" Foundation from 2006, there are only 2100 Galapagos penguins left, which means there are only 1000 couples ready for reproduction according to the International Penguin Preservation Working Group.

Southern rockhopper penguin, Magellanic penguin and Humboldt penguin are threatened by mass commercial sardine fishing, while fisherman complain how penguins take significant quantity of possible catch, while the penguins on the other hand lose their basic food.

In general, penguins from Sphenicus order, i.e. Magellanic and Humboldt penguins on the costs of South America and nearby islands, jackass penguin on the Cape of Good Hope and Galapagos penguin are threatened by oil spills and in the last few years two large oil spills killed a large number of these penguins. Penguin that are threatened in this way can be caught, cleaned from oil and returned to sea, but it is a very expensive and long process usually performed by voluntary organizations (e.g. *SANCCOB, Defenders of Wildlife* etc.).

Most other species are relatively safe. However, they also face two main threats. The first threat are plans for commercial krill fishing on Antarctic, which could threaten all the species that feed on krill, as well as those that feed on fish that feeds on krill. The other threat is global warming, which will make the water warmer, thus making the penguins move more to the south in order to survive the climate changes. However, the problem with climate change is that it is happening to fast and it remains a big question if penguins will be able to adapt in time.

Penguins are adored by people, primarily for their upright stance, which resembles humans, and their waddling gait. Also, people love penguins because they, unlike other birds, are not afraid of humans. Penguins are often portrayed in cartoons wearing a white tie suit, due to specific colour of their feathers. Penguins have been subject of several animated pictures, such as Happy Feet and Surf's Up. Logo of the Linux operating system is a penguin named Tux.

People collect penguin eggs for food, since they are very tasty, while penguin meat is not edible. However, penguins are not afraid of humans and researchers can easily approach them. The reason is that humans have historically not been present in their habitat as predators. Penguins usually stay at a distance of about three meters, which is also a distance recommended to tourists: if penguins come closer, which often happens, there is no need to withdraw.

End of text. You can stop the stopwatch.

This text has exactly 2945 words.

You can calculate your average reading speed in the following manner: Divide the number of words in this text (2945) with the time it took you to read it measured in seconds, then multiply the result by 60. You will get an average number of words read per minute.

Now try and answer the following 10 questions about the segment you just read.

1. Where do penguins mostly live?

    a) In the Northern Hemisphere
    b) In the Eastern Hemisphere
    c) In the Southern Hemisphere
    d) In the Western Hemisphere

2. How much of their lives do penguins spend in water?

    a) One third of their life
    b) Half of their life
    c) Slightly more than a half of their life
    d) Most of their life

3. What is the name of the largest and at the same time the heaviest penguin species?

    a) Jackass penguin
    b) Emperor penguin
    c) Galapagos penguin
    d) King penguin

4. How much time can penguins spend underwater?

a) Up to 10 minutes
b) Up to 20 minutes
c) Up to 25 minutes
d) Up to 30 minutes

5. How much does the smallest penguin species, so called little blue penguin weigh?

    a) Around 1 kg
    b) Around 2 kg
    c) Around 5 kg
    d) Around 10 kg

6. Can penguins see ultraviolet wavelength?

    a) yes
    b) no
    c) probably

7. Compared to other bird species, penguins hearing is:

    a) Better
    b) Worse
    c) The same as in the other birds

8. How thick is a fat layer of a penguin?

    a) Up to 1 cm
    b) Up to 3 cm
    c) Up to 5 cm
    d) Up to 10 cm

9. What is an average lifespan of a penguin?

    a) 3 to 5 years
    b) 5 to 10 years

c) 15 to 20 years
d) 20 to 25 years

10. There were several million jackass penguins 100 years ago, but now there are only:

a) Around 20.000
b) Around 50.000
c) Around 100.000
d) Around 500.000

Answers can be found on the next page. You can easily calculate your success rate. For example, if you had six correct answers it means your level of comprehension is 60%, if you had three correct - 30%, etc.

Answers: 1c, 2b, 3b, 4b, 5a, 6c, 7c, 8b, 9c, 10b

Punctuation marks and reading by segments

Did you know that average comprehension level is just 55%? This might seem a bit low, but these are the results of the latest studies. The goal of this book, in addition to improving your reading speed is also to improve your level of comprehension. You will find that punctuation marks are very helpful:

! – exclamation mark
? – question mark
. – full stop
, – comma

Very often a text and the sentences of a text contain several separate segments of meaning. Let's look at the following sentence, for example.

The fall of the apple from the tree,   caused by severe storm,
lasted for entire minute   since the tree was on the edge of a cliff which is considered to be one of the biggest cliffs in Europe.

You will notice that a split sentence is much easier to understand than the following, joined sentence:

The fall of the apple from the tree, caused by severe storm lasted for entire minute since the tree was on the edge of a cliff which is considered to be one of the biggest cliffs in Europe.

When reading, it is much easier to understand the text if you group words into segments of meaning. Your level of comprehension and ability to remember what you just read will increase if you use this method. So, when reading, try and put more attention to punctuation marks and meaningful segments. After a period of adjustment, this technique will help you to improve comprehension and to have better memory of the text you read.

Numbers can also be used as a good example. Look at these nine figures:

528645942

It is not easy to remember such long series of numbers. However, if we group the numbers we get:

528   645   942

You will agree that this is now much easier to memorize. This technique can be used for words in a sentence as well. My advice is that you should try and develop a habit of dividing a text into segments of meaning. Thus, it will become easier to comprehend, and at the same time you will be able to increase your reading speed.

You would probably be surprised to learn that an average adult comprehends only about 55% of text read. There are several reasons that cause difficulties regarding comprehension. A text can sometimes be full of information we are unable to immediately comprehend, sometimes the material is too technical, and sometimes we have trouble concentrating. All these put together can significantly decrease our comprehension level, while we remain almost completely unaware of that.

Most of these problems can be solved by improving the reading speed. Some readers will probably ask themselves: *If I already have trouble comprehending a text, how can higher reading speed improve my level of comprehension?*

I had similar thoughts in the beginning. I remember how teachers used to say to us "Kids, read slowly and with understanding". This advice is, truth be told, useful for school kids who are learning how to read. On the other hand, in case of adult readers, it only leads to worse comprehension and slower reading.

So, with speed reading:
– your concentration grows, since you are always required to follow the meaning of a text;
– you are quicker to observe segments of meaning, beginning and the end of a sentence wrote by the author;
– you quickly go over unimportant information and get a broader picture;
– save your time and have the ability to cover larger amount of text at a same time.

If you are sceptical, you can test this theory for yourself. Take the most difficult, most technical text and read it as fast as you can. You will see that these advices make sense. By the way, you don't have to read every word, you are even allowed to skip a few of them.

Look at this example:

The fall of the apple from the trxx,
 caused by sevxxx storm,
lasted xxx xxxxxx minute
xxxxx the tree was on the edge of a clixx
which is considered xx xxx of the biggest cliffs in Europe.

As you can see from this example, you can read just 60% of words while retaining full comprehension of the text.

I had an interesting experience while listening to books in foreign language on Amazon's Audible platform. As I listened to the book *Mann ohne Eigenschaften,* I heard many new German words and idioms that were unknown to me. Since I am not a native speaker of German language, I was very surprised with the fact that I was able to improve text comprehension by increasing the speed of listening. In my personal experience, I managed to improve comprehension by 30% when I increased listening speed from 1 to 1.5.

Although I was surprised in the beginning, I soon realized that some sentences can get very long and that by listening at higher speed it was easier for me to get the meaning and understand intentions of the author.

I advise you to try this for yourself. *Audible* application is free and offers many interesting books. You can try and listen books in a language other than your native language, because at the same time you can practice and improve your foreign language skills. In order to apply this advice, you should have at least B1 or B2 level of language skill.

The power of peripheral vision

There is a quote that perfectly fits here:
"A book is a great thing if a man knows how to use it" - Bloch
:)

In this chapter I will give brief explanation about how peripheral vision affects our speed reading ability. As you already know, peripheral vision is the ability of a person to see objects outside its narrow field of vision. In general, this means that we are aware of other objects in the environment, although we are not focused on them.

Our ability to see objects by our peripheral vision can be very successfully implemented to speed reading techniques. Most of the advanced techniques are actually based on use of peripheral vision. The method of reading by peripheral vision includes reading several groups of words at once.

Similar to the previously mentioned example:

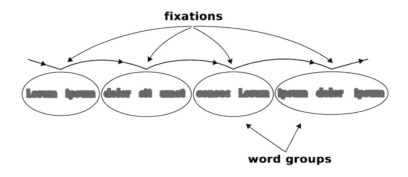

Human eye is capable of seeing several groups of words at the same time. When you become capable of reading in this way you can "expand" your focus on several words at once. Just try, for the sake of exercise, to point your eyes at a single word and then check your current ability of peripheral reading.

Let's take this sentence for example:

„This book will **help** me read much faster than I used to."

Now focus your eyes on the bolded word "help". Do not move your eyes from this word and check how many words, to the left and to the right of this word, you can see with your peripheral vision. On average, it is considered a good start if you can read only one word to the left and one word to the right. In a separate chapter of this book you will find exercises used to practice your peripheral vision.

Now try and practice the feeling of capturing several words at once. From this point on, try and look at the words from this peripheral perspective. This is how you begin practicing your peripheral vision. Peripheral vision helped me progress much faster and made my speed reading exercises much easier.

Here's a look at an average fixation pattern if peripheral vision is not used:

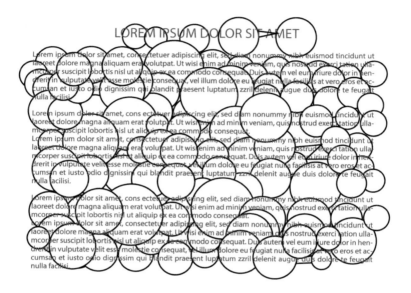

In this example, peripheral vision is not used and this causes a large number of fixations, which indirectly causes a very slow reading speed.

Now see how the same text looks when trained peripheral vision is used.

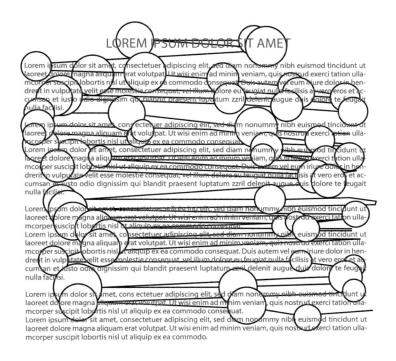

Here you can see that number of fixations is much lower than before. The goal of the exercises found at the end of the book is to develop the ability to see text in this way.

Once you master the technique of peripheral reading, you can expect to achieve two or three times faster reading speed. It is not unusual for the fastest readers in the world to be able to see up to 10 or more words at once, which is the result of many years of training. Your starting goal is to see 2-3 words at once and to progressively develop your ability to read groups of words.

An interesting fact about peripheral vision is that it can also be practiced vertically. When looking at a single word, you are also capable of seeing the word above it and the word below it. In practice, this means that there are some people capable of reading two or more lines at ones. It all depends on how much you developed this reading technique. Their view of the text is similar to the following example:

Lorem ipsum

Lorem ipsum dolor sit amet, consectetuer adipiscing elit, sed diam nonummy nibh euismod tincidunt ut laoreet dolore magna aliquam erat volutpat. Ut wisi enim ad minim veniam, quis nostrud exerci tation ullamcorper suscipit lobortis nisl ut aliquip ex ea commodo consequat. Duis autem vel eum iriure dolor in hendrerit in vulputate velit esse molestie consequat, vel illum dolore eu feugiat nulla facilisis at vero eros et accumsan et iusto odio dignissim qui blandit praesent luptatum zzril delenit.v

Lorem ipsum dolor sit amet, cons ectetuer adipiscing elit, sed diam nonummy nibh euismod tincidunt ut laoreet dolore magna aliquam erat volutpat. Ut wisi enim ad minim veniam, quis nostrud exerci tation ullamcorper suscipit lobortis nisl ut aliquip ex ea commodo consequat.

In the picture above, you can see that arrows don't start from the beginning of a line and they don't end with the line. Also, the eye traces every second row. The reason for this is use of both vertical and horizontal vision.

So, depending on your abilities and how much time you spent practicing, you will over time become capable of reading two or more rows at once. You will begin reading from the third or the fourth word in a line and end on the third or the fourth word from the end. You will see the first and the last word by your peripheral vision.

Some of the best readers in the world use the ability of peripheral vision combined with backwards reading. Let's see how your eye is supposed to move over a page:

Lorem ipsum

Lorem ipsum dolor sit amet, consectetuer adipiscing elit, sed diam nonummy nibh euismod tincidunt ut laoreet dolore magna aliquam erat volutpat. Ut wisi enim ad minim veniam, quis nostrud exerci tation ullamcorper suscipit lobortis nisl ut aliquip ex ea commodo consequat. Duis autem vel eum iriure dolor in hendrerit in vulputate velit esse molestie consequat, vel illum dolore eu feugiat nulla facilisis at vero eros et accumsan et iusto luptatum. Lorem ipsum dolor sit amet, cons ectetuer adipiscing elit, sed diam nonummy nibh euismod tincidunt u

Lorem ipsum dolor sit amet, cons ectetuer adipiscing elit, sed diam nonummy nibh euismod tincidunt ut laoreet dolore magna aliquam erat volutpat. Ut wisi enim ad minim veniam, quis nostrud exerci tation ullamcorper suscipit lobortis nisl ut aliquip ex velit esse molestie consequat, vel illum dolore eros et.

To sum this chapter up:
– peripheral vision is extremely useful for speed reading;
– peripheral vision means reading of word groups at once;
– peripheral vision includes both horizontal and vertical vision;
– peripheral vision can be improved by exercising.

Advanced meta-guiding techniques

After a while, when you get used to using a guide as a visual aid and after you develop your peripheral vision, then is the time to start practicing the advanced techniques. Advanced meta-guiding techniques (AMGT) allow you to increase you reading speed several times. In order to master them, you'll have to put even more effort and to practice even more. In the beginning, you will find these exercises to be very hard to master, but don't let that discourage you. Just practice regularly and be persistent and soon you will be making small steps towards mastering them.

The most commonly used meta-guiding techniques are:

– the double line sweep;

– the variable sweep and

– the reverse sweep.

The double line sweep means reading two lines of text at the same time. This technique is not much different from the original pen tracing technique, only that now you are practicing with two instead of one line at a time.

This technique is also used as an exercise for your peripheral vision. It is important to exercise both your horizontal and vertical vision. Once you develop the peripheral vision, you will feel great. The feeling of being able to read two or more lines at once for the first time is amazing. The feeling is similar to the one of learning how to swim or how to ride a bike. Besides being time-saving, this technique also causes less fatigue to the eye. Also, it is not the same if you can read two lines at once or if you have to read each line individually. The picture below shows how double line sweep looks:

> Speed reading is any of several techniques used to improve one's ability to read quickly. Speed reading methods include chunking and minimizing subvocalization. The many available speed reading training programs include books, videos, software, and seminars.
>
> Psychologists and educational specialists working on visual acuity used a tachistoscope to conclude,[1] that with training, an average person could identify minute images flashed on the screen for only one five-hundredth of a second (2 ms). Though the images used were of airplanes, the results had implications for reading. [2]
>
> It was not until the late 1950s that a portable, reliable and convenient device would be developed as a tool for increasing reading speed. Evelyn Wood, a researcher and schoolteacher, was committed to understanding why some people were naturally faster at reading and tried to force herself to read very quickly. In 1958, while brushing off the pages of a book she had thrown down in despair, she discovered that the sweeping motion of her hand across the page caught the attention of her eyes, and helped them move more smoothly across the page. She then used the hand as a pacer. Wood first taught the method at the University of Utah, before launching it to the public as Evelyn Wood's Reading Dynamics in Washington, D.C. in 1959.[3]
>
> Skimming is a process of speed reading that involves visually searching the sentences of a page for clues to meaning. Or when reading an essay, it can mean reading the beginning and ending for summary information, then optionally the first sentence of each paragraph to quickly determine whether to seek still more detail, as determined by the questions or purpose of the reading.[4][5][6][7][8] For some people, this comes naturally, but is usually acquired by practice. Skimming is usually seen more in adults than in children. It is conducted at a higher rate (700 words per minute and above) than normal reading for comprehension (around 200–230 wpm), and results in lower comprehension rates,[9] especially with information-

Once you master this technique, you can start practicing how to read two lines at once.

Musicians are in advantage when it comes to learning this technique. Due to being used to vertical writing and reading of the notes, the musicians are somewhat more comfortable with this technique.

The variable sweep means reading several lines at a time. The best readers are capable of reading up to eight lines per each sweep. This practically multiplies their reading speed. For a start, try using this technique on two lines and then progressively increase the number of lines you read.

> Speed reading is any of several techniques used to improve one's ability to read quickly. Speed reading methods include chunking and minimizing subvocalization. The many available speed reading training programs include books, videos, software, and seminars.
>
> Psychologists and educational specialists working on visual acuity used a tachistoscope to conclude,[1] that with training, an average person could identify minute images flashed on the screen for only one five-hundredth of a second (2 ms). Though the images used were of airplanes, the results had implications for reading.[2]
>
> It was not until the late 1950s that a portable, reliable and convenient device would be developed as a tool for increasing reading speed. Evelyn Wood, a researcher and schoolteacher, was committed to understanding why some people were naturally faster at reading and tried to force herself to read very quickly. In 1958, while brushing off the pages of a book she had thrown down in despair, she discovered that the sweeping motion of her hand across the page caught the attention of her eyes, and helped them move more smoothly across the page. She then used the hand as a pacer. Wood first taught the method at the University of Utah, before launching it to the public as Evelyn Wood's Reading Dynamics in Washington, D.C. in 1959.[3]
>
> Skimming is a process of speed reading that involves visually searching the sentences of a page for clues to meaning. Or when reading an essay, it can mean reading the beginning and ending for summary information, then optionally the first sentence of each paragraph to quickly determine whether to seek still more detail, as determined by the questions or purpose of the reading.[4][5][6][7][8] For some people, this comes naturally, but is usually acquired by practice. Skimming is usually seen more in adults than in children. It is conducted at a higher rate (700 words per minute and above) than normal reading for comprehension (around 200–230 wpm), and results in lower comprehension rates,[9] especially with information-

Our peripheral vision makes this possible. In this case, the success depends on the amount of practice. If you start thinking that you can't achieve this and you want to quit, just ask yourself: "If there are people capable of reading eight lines at a time, why shouldn't I be able of reading at least two or three?". This way of thinking can motivate you and encourage you to continue with practice.

The reverse sweep means backward reading of a text. It may sound unusual, but there are entire languages and their alphabets that are written and read from right to left. The following example shows how backward reading improves the reading speed. You can explain this technique through a metaphor of sweeping snow from a street using a large snow shovel. You can do this by always starting on the lefts side of a street and pushing the snow to the right. However, you will lose half the time returning to the left side, where you can start sweeping the next row. Get it? The goal is to learn to read a text from right to left. By mastering this technique, you can significantly improve your reading speed.

> Speed reading is any of several techniques used to improve one's ability to read quickly. Speed reading methods include chunking and minimizing subvocalization. The many available speed reading training programs include books, videos, software, and seminars.
>
> Psychologists and educational specialists working on visual acuity used a tachistoscope to conclude,[1] that with training, an average person could identify minute images flashed on the screen for only one-five-hundredth of a second (2 ms). Though the images used were of airplanes, the results had implications for reading. [2]
>
> It was not until the late 1950s that a portable, reliable and convenient device would be developed as a tool for increasing reading speed. Evelyn Wood, a researcher and schoolteacher, was committed to understanding why some people were naturally faster at reading and tried to force herself to read very quickly. In 1958, while brushing off the pages of a book she had thrown down in despair, she discovered that the sweeping motion of her hand across the page caught the attention of her eyes, and helped them move more smoothly across the page. She then used the hand as a pacer. Wood first taught the method at the University of Utah, before launching it to the public as Evelyn Wood's Reading Dynamics in Washington, D.C. in 1959.[3]
>
> Skimming is a process of speed reading that involves visually searching the sentences of a page for clues to meaning. Or when reading an essay, it can mean reading the beginning and ending for summary information, then optionally the first sentence of each paragraph to quickly determine whether to seek still more detail, as determined by the questions or purpose of the reading.[4][5][6][7][8] For some people, this comes naturally, but is usually acquired by practice. Skimming is usually seen more in adults than in children. It is conducted at a higher rate (700 words per minute and above) than normal reading for comprehension (around 200–230 wpm), and results in lower comprehension rates,[9] especially with information-

You can look at the text as if it was a giant puzzle. The brain is the one responsible for connecting the pieces together and giving them meaning.

For example, one long sentences can take up to five or more lines. It occasionally happens that the last 2-3 words determine the meaning of all the above lines. Your brain was actually on hold while you read the lines and started processing the information only after you read the entire sentence. The same thing happens with double line, variable and reverse sweep. You only have to train your brain to more easily and more quickly connect the words into comprehensible and logical blocks.

Advanced visual guiding movements

Specific visual guiding movements have been developed to help you train your peripheral vision:
– the vertical wave;
– the "S";
– the "Z";
– the zig-zag;
– the loop;
– the double guide.

The goal is that you use a guide or other visual aid to trace the text on the page following a present path. This book explains the six most common movements used by speed readers. I advise you to try each one of them and find the one that suits you the most.

A) The vertical wave

The idea is to focus your eyes in the middle section and slowly glide it to the sentence below. Slight movements to the left and to the right are allowed as you advance through the text. Sometimes, in case of books of large format it is impossible to see all the information which is not placed in the centre. You should try and cover as large as possible groups of words and use the peripheral vision to read words to the left and to the right from the middle of a line.

> Speed reading is any of several techniques used to improve one's ability to read quickly. Speed reading methods include chunking and minimizing subvocalization. The many available speed reading training programs include books, videos, software, and seminars.
>
> Psychologists and educational specialists working on visual acuity used a tachistoscope to conclude,[1] that with training, an average person could identify minute images flashed on the screen for only one five-hundredth of a second (2 ms). Though the images used were of airplanes, the results had implications for reading. [2]
>
> It was not until the late 1950s that a portable, reliable and convenient device would be developed as a tool for increasing reading speed. Evelyn Wood, a researcher and schoolteacher, was committed to understanding why some people were naturally faster at reading and tried to force herself to read very quickly. In 1958, while brushing off the pages of a book she had thrown down in despair, she discovered that the sweeping motion of her hand across the page caught the attention of her eyes, and helped them move more smoothly across the page. She then used the hand as a pacer. Wood first taught the method at the University of Utah, before launching it to the public as Evelyn Wood's Reading Dynamics in Washington, D.C. in 1959.[3]
>
> Skimming is a process of speed reading that involves visually searching the sentences of a page for clues to meaning. Or when reading an essay, it can mean reading the beginning and ending for summary information, then optionally the first sentence of each paragraph to quickly determine whether to seek still more detail, as determined by the questions or purpose of the reading.[4][5][6][7][8] For some people, this comes naturally, but is usually acquired by practice. Skimming is usually seen more in adults than in children. It is conducted at a higher rate (700 words per minute and above) than normal reading for comprehension (around 200–230 wpm), and results in lower comprehension rates,[9] especially with information-

In time, as you develop the horizontal vision, the need to move slightly to the left and to the right will gradually diminish. The idea of this method is that after some time you become able of reading an entire line by looking only at its middle section. Including the words in the left and in the right section. Once you are capable of doing that, you can simply trace a guide through the middle section of a page from top to bottom.

b) The "S"

This technique is considered to be one of the most advanced and the most difficult to master. In order to start using this movement, you must first master the following techniques:
– variable sweep;
– backward reading and
– peripheral vision.

This technique combines all three methods. Just look at the S shape and you'll realize why.

c) The "Z"

This technique is much easier to master than the previous one. Backward reading is not that much used, because there is only one backward line. But, truth be told, with a wider arc. In order to successfully complete this exercise, it would be very useful to develop the peripheral vision before you start.

d) The zig-zag

The zig-zag is one of the most advanced techniques. It requires variable sweep and reverse sweep. Use of peripheral vision is also necessary.
In this method you trace a visual aid to the margin, where you make a loop and proceed below and diagonally to the margin on the other side.

The advantage of this method is that it gives certain pace to your reading technique, thus improving duration and quality of your concentration.

e) The loop

The loop is very similar to the zig-zag technique. The only difference is in the size of the loop. In this case it is much bigger. In practice, this allows you to cover larger parts of text by peripheral vision.

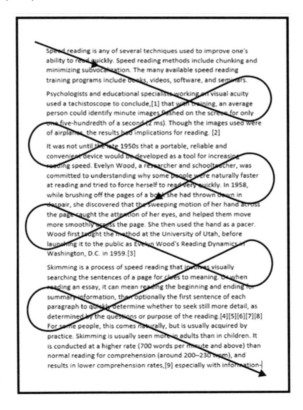

This is one of the favourite techniques of speed readers.

f) The double guide

This method requires use of two visual reading aids. Usually, you can use a guide or a pen on one side and your finger on the other. This technique allows you to absorb the text in between them while gradually progressing to the bottom of the page. In time, as you become more experienced, you will move faster towards the bottom of the page. Peripheral vision is used a lot for this technique.

Speed reading is any of several techniques used to improve one's ability to read quickly. Speed reading methods include chunking and minimizing subvocalization. The many available speed reading training programs include books, videos, software, and seminars.

Psychologists and educational specialists working on visual acuity used a tachistoscope to conclude,[1] that with training, an average person could identify minute images flashed on the screen for only one five-hundredth of a second (2 ms). Though the images used were of airplanes, the results had implications for reading. [2]

It was not until the late 1950s that a portable, reliable and convenient device would be developed as a tool for increasing reading speed. Evelyn Wood, a researcher and schoolteacher, was committed to understanding why some people were naturally faster at reading and tried to force herself to read very quickly. In 1958, while brushing off the pages of a book she had thrown down in despair, she discovered that the sweeping motion of her hand across the page caught the attention of her eyes, and helped them move more smoothly across the page. She then used the hand as a pacer. Wood first taught the method at the University of Utah, before launching it to the public as Evelyn Wood's Reading Dynamics in Washington, D.C. in 1959.[3]

Skimming is a process of speed reading that involves visually searching the sentences of a page for clues to meaning. Or when reading an essay, it can mean reading the beginning and ending for summary information, then optionally the first sentence of each paragraph to quickly determine whether to seek still more detail, as determined by the questions or purpose of the reading.[4][5][6][7][8] For some people, this comes naturally, but is usually acquired by practice. Skimming is usually seen more in adults than in children. It is conducted at a higher rate (700 words per minute and above) than normal reading for comprehension (around 200–230 wpm), and results in lower comprehension rates,[9] especially with information-

For a start, when you practice, read one line at a time, until you become capable of reading several lines at a time.

Exercises and Practice

Exercises for developing peripheral vision and perception

Exercises for vertical vision

The following exercises will help you develop the ability to read using the peripheral vision. The aim of these exercises is to expand your field of perception.

It is interesting that these exercises have first been developed for army and pilot training. Military studies showed that regular exercises help pilots become capable of more easily and quickly recognize friendly aircrafts from the enemy aircrafts. Decisions are often made in split second when the spotted aircraft is just a miniature spot in the peripheral field of vision.

For this exercise you will need a small 8x5 cm plastic card. It is recommended to use a white card so it doesn't present a distraction. Anyway, an ID card or payment card may serve the purpose. Here is how this exercise is done:

– use the card to cover the first two numbers (in this example, numbers 48 and 32);

– quickly move the card to reveal the numbers for a split second and then cover them again;

– try and guess the numbers;

– move to the next group of numbers and repeat the procedure.

The goal of this exercise is to observe information that is shown for a brief period of time only. This exercise will help you develop the ability of reading words that have been exposed for a split second.

Change the speed at which you cover and reveal the numbers, so that you are never 100% certain what you have just read. This is an exercise, so there is no use in slowly covering and revealing the number. So, use the highest possible speed at which you can correctly guess at least 50% of numbers.

Start the practice with four numbers, then with five, six and finally eight.

	48			80	
	32			32	

	33			13	
	22			47	

	86			84	
	48			41	

	83			52	
	37			80	

	84			59	
	63			40	

	95			65	
	32			43	

	80			43	
	14			22	

	71			58	
	44			83	

	66			95	
	25			68	

	71			33	
	82			84	

	92			91	
	88			32	

	39			47	
	13			95	

	33			50	
	49			88	

	76			41	
	47			89	

	10			14	
	64			65	

	28			69	
	72			39	

	54			49	
	36			93	

	21			20	
	21			24	

	13			21	
	38			35	

	73			51	
	73			29	

	62			89	
	622			421	

	40			22	
	125			225	

```
     25              58
    849             483
_____     _____

     38              32
    273             100
_____     _____


     63              65
    793             251
_____     _____

     45              50
    984             105
_____     _____

     75              78
    673             968
_____     _____

     16              87
    352             661
_____     _____

     85              79
    916             994
_____     _____

     48              62
    572             869
_____     _____

     26              19
    654             400
_____     _____
```

| 67 | | 75 |
| 229 | | 675 |

| 79 | | 64 |
| 859 | | 587 |

| 13 | | 22 |
| 814 | | 869 |

| 26 | | 39 |
| 128 | | 163 |

| 99 | | 64 |
| 145 | | 111 |

| 86 | | 48 |
| 793 | | 661 |

| 24 | | 19 |
| 729 | | 153 |

| 56 | | 12 |
| 609 | | 141 |

| 55 | | 54 |
| 903 | | 528 |

| | 990 | | | 101 | |
| | 699 | | | 370 | |

| | 601 | | | 215 | |
| | 481 | | | 161 | |

| | 361 | | | 130 | |
| | 500 | | | 591 | |

| | 700 | | | 791 | |
| | 744 | | | 776 | |

| | 818 | | | 433 | |
| | 423 | | | 222 | |

| | 889 | | | 958 | |
| | 645 | | | 677 | |

| | 774 | | | 320 | |
| | 572 | | | 464 | |

| | 756 | | | 935 | |
| | 818 | | | 661 | |

| | 174 | | | 338 | |
| | 761 | | | 316 | |

667		435	
178		526	

178		867	
431		171	

186		923	
674		200	

611		543	
572		381	

911		617	
715		404	

913		103	
941		203	

878		956	
490		471	

837		775	
147		243	

993		935	
746		272	

784 + 988 =	592 + 150 =
363 + 858 =	313 + 932 =
3993 + 3731 =	5742 + 3323 =
7332 + 6267 =	8817 + 8881 =
8410 + 4788 =	3802 + 1603 =
1394 + 8182 =	6249 + 2434 =
1759 + 5281 =	2188 + 7734 =
7434 + 3961 =	3560 + 3370 =
4051 + 6847 =	3133 + 3111 =

| 6359 | | 7070 | |
| 4251 | | 8189 | |

| 1695 | | 2911 | |
| 7530 | | 6319 | |

| 4244 | | 6730 | |
| 2875 | | 8062 | |

| 4404 | | 6799 | |
| 6287 | | 5913 | |

| 4472 | | 8197 | |
| 8165 | | 3638 | |

| 9055 | | 6480 | |
| 3404 | | 8868 | |

| 9277 | | 4590 | |
| 4040 | | 8816 | |

| 3451 | | 1843 | |
| 8698 | | 8364 | |

| 7638 | | 6376 | |
| 6352 | | 7666 | |

	4236		4723
_____	7261	_____	3477	_____

	6418		9185
_____	1744	_____	3726	_____

	8600		5009
_____	1632	_____	2136	_____

	5852		8031
_____	5291	_____	3235	_____

	4851		4030
_____	7442	_____	3590	_____

	9758		4761
_____	4275	_____	5297	_____

Exercises for horizontal vision

This next exercise will help you develop your horizontal vision. Below you will find numbers written in several lines. Your task is to read the first number and then find the same number in the line as quickly as you can. Try to do this as fast as you can and to catch as much number groups as possible with your sight.

56	24	54	53	93	56	66	80
23	38	23	90	24	37	98	60

58	19	25	18	58	64	41	95
88	16	49	79	19	16	52	88
60	52	60	33	29	74	24	97
22	82	33	97	70	50	83	22
38	76	13	38	62	22	22	49
92	23	81	39	33	57	92	88
34	72	92	60	45	51	32	34
47	42	66	18	48	83	47	87
62	43	42	84	84	35	62	77
35	21	62	81	35	47	72	89
41	16	44	40	48	41	81	84
58	41	48	51	48	64	61	58
75	61	71	67	69	96	75	16
89	89	96	15	90	84	93	71
37	18	22	92	75	54	37	46
35	96	53	63	90	74	23	35
25	36	25	12	30	50	11	60
13	17	81	97	13	65	29	80
21	40	22	16	21	87	81	39
83	92	83	49	29	73	53	58
30	38	35	17	39	24	95	30
74	17	91	46	78	74	90	81
56	57	30	61	25	56	28	59
48	23	18	44	56	48	68	99
95	85	67	49	92	95	68	47
17	17	42	56	61	96	56	96
69	83	68	32	52	66	85	69
95	41	46	31	95	44	49	35
920	909	920	915	291	598	714	342
998	163	694	689	998	669	157	367

914	932	914	273	676	562	242	407
599	596	720	363	214	547	357	599
735	242	572	342	725	735	445	507
981	981	301	124	596	558	981	593
898	435	898	846	266	486	993	343
743	964	352	386	386	970	743	317
488	549	750	488	810	770	373	410
240	227	759	338	156	240	393	682
392	573	497	439	678	989	640	392
998	822	655	784	723	920	998	676
390	934	390	235	160	146	582	362
735	363	231	539	958	735	870	485
588	588	733	567	255	968	245	593
517	162	249	517	134	861	214	683
240	734	552	147	657	240	959	361
539	723	865	619	557	926	714	539
850	709	468	116	307	395	850	946
202	634	202	907	798	961	624	322
933	742	800	393	933	960	289	415
493	493	556	564	648	837	186	863
285	778	936	933	611	285	508	251
698	980	253	478	813	515	698	890
154	154	308	971	308	884	811	987
685	976	396	982	977	685	336	793
238	437	983	879	156	118	234	405
530	865	151	238	620	894	530	355
932	649	239	619	150	246	932	871
212	289	212	981	351	476	626	347
292	201	458	945	311	579	292	790
463	323	463	216	272	327	247	659
128	460	107	961	623	729	128	638
605	605	249	256	598	576	250	995
247	792	688	678	352	693	881	247

823	743	428	234	394	823	704	144
989	175	989	612	834	603	456	865
963	389	954	800	599	432	463	963
450	447	521	453	253	450	783	413
837	441	714	932	813	364	837	597
734	426	771	804	734	624	371	983
669	318	822	888	683	593	669	673
508	508	891	789	172	252	367	295
500	853	500	760	834	354	396	355
353	567	677	962	479	726	649	353
816	803	388	816	623	248	890	917
115	216	115	680	346	876	728	856
408	896	153	408	788	529	484	824
862	725	282	702	592	102	989	862
842	118	842	503	737	776	984	513

3515	7817	9340	8003	3515	7397	3007	8189
7010	1986	1177	7010	2269	2292	5385	2843
9037	9037	1699	3510	2060	1760	1082	8798
9087	6385	6074	6979	4249	5790	3383	9087
1183	9353	7233	1183	4323	6576	3891	1357
6670	3116	6100	4586	8058	6670	2838	7320
6135	6135	3918	5351	2021	1941	1480	9503
8895	8813	2741	2372	4610	3644	8895	6169
8646	5757	2963	8646	5934	2518	5493	9363
3243	4827	7475	7427	5282	5761	3243	2025
8096	2251	8069	1184	9792	8408	8096	5845
5026	7885	5023	3008	7525	5026	9465	9284
4461	4461	1590	2434	4462	7018	2873	2432
8406	4868	8604	3108	4509	4608	8406	4631

9358	8545	9583	1292	5225	9358	2915	4409
5538	8927	3785	5232	4763	2472	5538	9860
4443	1632	4443	8963	9853	6564	3286	4186
3872	4467	3871	3324	3872	4886	8841	8655
9033	5350	6456	7931	6089	9033	8114	9460
8226	1180	7784	9310	8226	1613	5391	4048
8410	3467	8419	3536	8930	8410	2440	1015
5092	6162	7173	1121	7175	5629	5092	3443
7459	8369	2385	7459	3222	3417	7138	9745
2487	2487	7509	9751	8779	8330	6046	4379
4514	4973	7393	8228	3005	5661	4063	4514
1684	1229	7433	1684	7370	8206	2573	3619
8830	4203	5139	2107	8040	6949	8830	6515
8742	9059	8742	6571	2054	4999	9891	5720
2777	5096	7994	2724	6453	2777	2935	5102
7225	9205	6330	7225	9300	4278	4677	6477
5912	4355	8744	9784	5319	5912	9096	5800
4345	4345	8912	9821	5504	2165	3599	4167
1323	1888	5400	4459	6471	1134	1721	1323
5119	9290	1488	5495	6185	5119	3798	1046
4522	6004	4522	7519	3039	9568	1762	5133
6533	5103	7863	1004	4296	4340	6533	7530
6007	3524	2695	1917	5869	6976	7371	6007
1212	7339	4533	1212	8818	1122	4134	8940
8578	3467	5553	8429	8578	2542	9890	5486
8460	5990	8460	1555	8392	7850	5586	6531
1692	3207	2456	1692	2209	3363	2503	9011
8910	8910	4112	4044	1061	6198	2556	1221
8553	3815	5353	2821	8782	8553	7199	3642
7651	7651	2051	2237	9431	3845	7842	2798
9133	5983	3011	6738	6083	5148	9398	9133
6526	9815	3187	7077	2541	1880	6526	1619
6166	3580	1842	7811	6166	1551	3131	3403

5912	5912	6600	4832	6546	1011	4374	7858
5304	1272	9416	4719	2294	5304	1280	5362
5247	2220	4786	1308	4336	8452	3253	5247
7244	3606	7244	9403	5021	3529	9894	1663
9584	1221	5883	3963	6392	9584	6782	5656
9739	7905	6484	2199	9739	2487	5314	3072
9436	4129	9436	4381	9748	3162	1174	2382
1614	1614	7239	3145	2616	7953	8411	3329
9100	9345	9100	6677	2858	7738	7988	7428
8143	1911	8142	1971	1935	8143	4683	9563
6815	4477	6811	1697	4896	2761	6815	7404
4390	6100	7600	4333	8873	5863	9789	4390
8175	9380	8805	8265	8358	8175	9213	5601

Subtitles exercise to help you quickly spot large groups of words

One of the main characteristic of slow readers is that they read word by word. In this exercise we will attempt to reduce this bad habit as much as it is possible. The goal of the exercise is to read four to eight new words with a single glance.

For this exercise you'll need a plastic card or similar object, because the exercise is similar to the previous one. Here is your task:

1. Use the card to quickly cover one or two lines of the text.
2. Try to internally repeat the word you briefly saw.

Start the exercise with one line, then gradually progress to two or more lines. If after some time you memorize the text, just make a new Word document that can be used to continue with the exercise.

This technique is also an introduction to double line sweep.

Don Quixote

is a masterpiece

of Spanish and world literature,

written by Miguel Cervantes.

It is the most published and

translated book

in the world after Bible.

It is considered a founding work

of Western literature

and one of the best

fiction works

of all time,

and the most important book

of the Spanish Golden Age.

The first volume

was published

in 1605 and

its full title was

The Ingenious Nobleman

Sir Quixote of La Mancha.

The second volume, titled

Volume Two of the

The Ingenious Nobleman

Sir Quixote of La Mancha.

was published in 1615.

The first volume

was published

in Madrid

at the expense of Francisco de Robles,

printed in the printing shop of

Juan de la Cuesta,

in the late 1604.

It was sold from January

1605 and contained numerous printer's errors

due to the speed required by

the publisher.

This edition has been reprinted

during the same year and in the same printing shop,

so there are actually

two different editions from 1605.

The book quickly became
very popular and

very soon there were
pirated editions printed in

Valencia and Lisbon.
It was then published in

Aragon and Portugal,
for which Robles bought

rights in February.

However, since

Cervantes reserved printing rights
for Castile only,

he had almost no benefit
from the popularity and numerous

editions of his work. By August
1605 two editions were

already published in Madrid and two in Lisbon,
as well as one in Valencia. In 1607

one edition was published in Brussel,
and in 1608 Robles printed

one more edition in Madrid.
In 1610 an Italian edition

appeared, and one more
edition was printed in Brussel in 1611.

The first edition of the second volume
was printed in the same printing shop

that printed the first volume,
in late 1615.

Very soon
the same edition was printed in

Brussel and Valencia (1616)
and Lisbon (1617).

The edition containing
both first and second volume

was first published
in Barcelona in 1617.

It is assumed that
the idea of a middle-aged

nobleman who loses his sanity
after reading so many chivalry romances actually

isn't new and that
it probably first appeared

in one of
Cervantes' Exemplary

Novellas under
the title

Ingenious Nobleman of La Mancha
and the novel is

actually, an expanded version
of the novella which,

in the words of
Cervantes himself in the prologue

to the first volume,
was created during one

of his stints in
prison.

This assumption
arises from the allusions to

the great popularity of this work
which can be found in

Cervantes' contemporaries
such as Francisco Lopez

De Ubeda and Lope da Vega.
In 1920 Ramon Menendes and

Pidal, a renowned Spanish philologist,
historian and folklorist,

presented his theory
about how Cervantes found

inspiration for this work
in the Entremes de los romances

by unknown author
which speaks about

a peasant who falls mad due to

excessive reading of chivalric ballads and

decides to leave his wife and,
like Don Quixote,

start an adventure as
a wondering knight who

fights injustice,
protects the weak and saves virgins.

Schulte grid for peripheral vision practice

German psychotherapist and psychiatrist Walter Schulte designed a useful system for development and training of peripheral vision.

Below you will find three tables containing numbers. Here is what you are supposed to do:

1. Focus on the grid centre. In the first grid, it is the position between numbers 4, 14, 7 and 16.
2. Without moving your eyes try and find all the numbers with your peripheral vision. Start from number 1 and finish on number 16.
3. When you find the number, briefly put the tip of your pen to the field and continue until you reach the final number.
4. After finding all numbers, move the tip of the pen outside the grid.

5. Measure how much time you need to finish the entire grid.

Expected time for this grid is 16 seconds. General rule is that the amount of time in seconds is equal to the number of fields.
Once you are able to complete a grid in 20% less time, you can move to a more complex one.

Schulte grid with 16 fields (4x4)

6	10	3	12
1	4	14	8
13	7	16	11
15	9	5	2

Schulte grid with 16 fields (4x4)

4	14	12	1
11	16	9	7
6	2	5	15
10	13	8	3

Schulte grid with 25 fields (5x5)

16	12	4	24	3
5	8	19	18	21
22	25	20	7	11
9	23	2	13	15
1	14	10	17	6

Schulte grid with 25 fields (5x5)

2	23	7	13	19
15	10	25	20	6
18	24	22	17	3
4	21	8	12	14
11	16	5	1	9

Schulte grid with 25 fields (5x5)

11	4	23	15	9
22	20	5	12	3
7	18	1	17	8
24	2	13	25	19
16	21	6	10	14

Schulte grid with 36 fields (6x6)

23	11	19	34	28	5
30	7	27	8	33	10
14	25	1	2	15	22
29	21	3	4	31	17
18	26	12	24	6	36
35	16	9	20	32	13

There is a very useful website with grids and a stopwatch that helps you measure the time: http://schulte-table.com/

There is also a mobile phone app, but I don't recommend it because of the small size of the screen.

Metronome as a reading aid

Many of you are not familiar with the word metronome. It is a device which produces sound in accurately defined periods of time. Today, you don't have to own the device. You can install an app on your phone or find a website that contains this feature for free.

Metronome can help you improve your reading speed. Set the metronome to 60 beats per minute. Use the visual aid while reading a text with a metronome ticking in the background. Every time you hear a "tick" put your pencil to the beginning of a new row. Is that time enough to read the text?

Adjust metronome speed based on your current reading speed. The goal of this exercise is to read faster with slightly lower level of comprehension. Number of metronome ticks should always be about 30% higher than your normal reading speed.

Your reading speed will be probably be somewhere in the range of 50 - 70 beats per minute. Then, in order for the exercise to have effect, you need to raise the metronome speed by 30%. Try to gradually increase metronome speed. Just a few notches every day will be enough. In time you will notice that metronome can also be useful to set the reading pace.

21-day exercise plan for developing and maintaining the reading speed

In this chapter you will find a three-week plan of exercises that have to be practiced every day. These exercises will not take more than 20 minutes a day and will allow you to quickly improve and master your reading techniques.

You need to put some effort into these exercises, stick to the plan and the results are inevitable. By the way, 2 - 3 times faster reading speed is a goal that is worthy of the effort.

You can continue with these exercises even after you complete the 21-day plan if you want to improve your reading speed even further.

In my experience, the reading speed achieved after the three-week exercise plan will not revert back to the previous level. However, I recommend you to repeat the 20-minute exercises once every month or every two months.

1. Number exercises – duration: 4 minutes

	48			80	
	32			32	
	33			13	
	22			47	

56	24	54	53	93	56	66	80
23	38	23	90	24	37	98	60

You will find numbers for this exercise in the Chapter "Exercises for developing the peripheral vision and perception". You can spend two minutes practicing with vertical and horizontal numbers, each.

Try to move from one line to another as quickly as possible. Principle of the exercise principle is explained in the chapter with numbers.

2. Subtitle exercises – duration: 3 minutes

Don Quixote

is a masterpiece

of Spanish and world literature,

written by Miguel Cervantes.

Practice for three minutes with subtitles. You will find the entire text for this exercise in Chapter "Exercises for developing the peripheral vision and perception".

3. Schulte grid exercises – duration: 3 minutes

6	10	3	12
1	4	14	8
13	7	16	11
15	9	5	2

Practice for three minutes with Schulte grids. You will find all the grids for this exercise in Chapter "Exercises for developing the peripheral vision and perception".

4. Reading at normal speed with visual aid - duration: 1 minute

This exercise is a warm-up for exercise 5. Pick any text and start reading while using a visual aid. Prepare the metronome app, because you will need it for the next exercise.

5. Reading with a metronome set to a speed that is 30% higher than your current reading speed - duration: 3 minutes

For this exercise, you will need a metronome. If you didn't manage to find the app, a free version available here: https://www.flutetunes.com/metronome/

The goal of this exercise is to read at a speed which is 30% faster than your normal reading speed. Therefore, your comprehension level will be somewhere between 50 and 60%.

Each time you here the beat you should move to the next line. Increase the metronome speed by 30% depending on your current reading speed and start the exercise. Set the application to just one tone and sound that suits you the most.

If you become aware that you can't understand at least 50% of the text at this speed, reduce the metronome speed by a notch.

With every new day increase the metronome speed by two beats.

Do not forget to always use the visual aid, not only when your practicing, but every time you're reading.

6. Reading with a metronome set to a speed that is 50% higher than your current reading speed - duration: 7 minutes

For this exercise you will have to increase the metronome speed by 20 beats compared to the previous exercise. Level of comprehension should be higher than 30%. Practice for 7 minutes.

With every day increase the metronome speed by two beats. When you reach 180 beats per minute, start with double line sweep, and set the metronome speed to 90 bpm. Continue increasing the rhythm by two beats every day. Decide by yourself what is the reading speed you want to accomplish.

It is not a mistake to use a text that you already familiar with for exercises 5 and 6.
Choose a material that is not too difficult.

By the way, these exercises are a sort of a conflict between reading speed, on one side, and comprehension, on the other. As you increase your reading speed, you will have more trouble with comprehension. That shouldn't discourage you. Our brain needs some time to adjust to processing the increased amount of information it receives. Anyway, if you continue with regular exercises your level of comprehension will certainly grow. In case you notice that you can't comprehend anything, reduce the speed. Practice is possible only if you have at least the slightest idea about the text meaning.

These exercises can be seen as a kind of gym for the brain. The same way certain athletes have a habit of visiting a gym every day to lift weights and practice their strength, these exercises are for your brain, speed reading and thinking.

Let me tell you about an interesting thing that happened to me after regular practicing the speed reading. I noticed that my ability of quick thinking improved. For example, someone is asking you a question and before he has even finished the sentence you already have three answers ready and you decide what is the right one. It feels like the time has stopped and you have additional 15 seconds to think about your answer, when in reality just 1-2 seconds have passed. :)

I think this is the result of processing huge amounts of information. Our brain has tremendous capacity, but without practice it becomes lazy and slow. So, just set the proper time for your exercises and after three weeks you will start noticing improvement in reading speed and your ability of quick thinking.

Set the goal - your desired reading speed

Every one of us has a certain motive or goal he wants to accomplish. Some of these goals are much more time consuming than the others. Speed reading techniques are not a skill that can be mastered in just a few days. You need to put in some effort and hard work. However, the results are very rewarding. Most of the participants increase their reading speed by two or three times and then stop. Some of them consider that to be enough.

My advice is that you should decide what your needs are. Do you want to spend several months practicing so you could read 10 times faster?

Ask yourself any of the following questions:
Why I want to read faster?
What reading speed I would be satisfied with?
How much time am I ready to spend on achieving this goal?
What improvements do I expect in my private and professional life?

The effort you put into practice should depend on how much the faster reading is important to you. My advice is to read as many books on this topic as you can, to attend speed reading seminars and to practice a little every day. The success is guaranteed. You just have to be persistent and keep trying. When you feel like you want to quit, ask yourself the following question: „How come some people can read 750 pages per hour, while I can barely read 50?". You are not less intelligent than that person. That person probably just spent more time developing its speed reading skills.

In the modern days you are required to process large quantity of information and to continuously improve yourself. If you wish to improve yourself, speed reading techniques will be of great help.

Bonus Chapter: How to Improve Your Memory?

In the next pages we will be talking about memory. This is a my gift to all the people who bought the book. This chapter will try to explain how our memory operates and it contains many useful tips on how to improve your memory. In addition to the interesting facts, in the end of the chapter you will find a few selected quotes.

This chapter has been added to the book because I think that speed reading techniques become the most efficient when used in combination with appropriate memory techniques.

The memory process can be explained as an activity which includes three steps: reception, memorization and retrieval of information. According to definition from expert literature it is "The process of conscious beings during which nervous system permanently or temporarily stores specific data". Through the history the memory has appeared as the result of evolution of nervous system of living creatures.

Did you know that our brain doesn't have a specific centre dedicated just for memory? Unlike activities such as speech, motor functions or hearing, memory centre is not separated. The memory process is actually a result of combined activities of several regions of the brain.

As for the energy usage, that is where our brain makes a convincing victory. With an average weight of just 1.5kg it manages to spend more than 20% of our total energy. It is interesting that in kids and babies, whose brains are still developing, this percentage can reach up to 60%.

People are capable of memorizing between five and nine items. Humans have the largest number of brain cells when they are 17, after which time their number starts to reduce. Dying of brain cells is a very slow and imperceptible process. On average, the people first start noticing that their memory is not as good as it used to be in their fifties. In practice, the degree to which our memory is preserved depends mostly on our lifestyle.

What types of memory are there?

Memory can be classified in different ways, but the traditional way of classification recognizes sensory, short-term and long-term memory. Classification is shown in detail on the following picture:

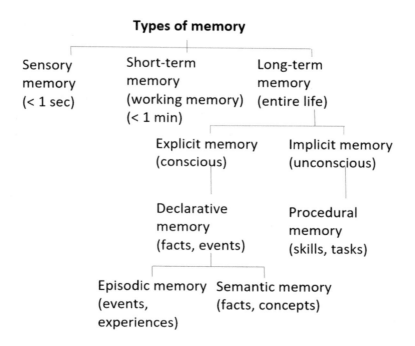

Sensory memory lasts the shortest, from a split second to several seconds on average. This type of memory can be described as an echo that remains after a certain action. For example: try to continuously repeat the number 324567. When you stop repeating, you won't be able to remember the number even after a few seconds. In practice, while you repeat the number, your sensory memory stores the information. When you stop repeating, the information is lost. Sensory memory is the guardian of our brain. Just imagine how difficult it would be for us to function if our brain were to remember every unimportant detail that happened to us during the day. For example: I checked the time at 3:30 p.m. Duration: two seconds. At the end of the day we would be buried in useless information, which would make it difficult to separate important from unimportant.

Let's look at one more example. Imagine you are in a bus in which 30 people are talking at the same time. When we don't listen to anyone, that's our sensory memory. When we focus on a conversation, that's when it our short-term memory turns on.

Short-term memory decides which information received from sensory memory is further processed. After 20 seconds to one minutes, this information disappears.

Long-term memory can last from few minutes, several years to a lifetime. The limit or capacity of the human brain for information is currently unknown. Forgetting protects our brain from being cluttered with excess information.

Long-term memory includes several processes:
– learning or decoding: the process of receiving new information;
– retrieving: consciousness or cognition of memorized information;
– consolidation or retention: consolidating information through repeated retrieval;
– creating connections between new and old information;
– forgetting: Loss of information or their change due to competitive new knowledge.

In order for information to get to the long-term memory, learning is required. During sleep our brain processes thoughts and places them into long-term memory. This process mostly take place during deep sleep. It is very common that persons that spend a lot of time learning during the day have longer periods of deep sleep during the night. This is the period during which our brain processes and stores new information. For example, if you study a lot during a day, there is a chance that deep sleep periods will last longer.

Explanation of memory process

Memory process can be depicted in the following way. Imagine an endless meadow with a lot of grass, plants and hills. There is a horse with a cart on that meadow. The path which the horse with a cart takes is hardly passable and the grass is high. In time, as it continues to take the same path again and again, cart tracks start to appear. After certain number of passings, it starts to look like a beaten path, i.e. a road.

Our memory operates in the similar way. First time you read something you need to learn, it leaves just a small mark in the memory or an echo of the entire text. The only safe way of long-term learning is to repeat the material several times in different time periods. According to the studies, after 24h we remember just 20% of the studied material.

Similar to the road that starts appearing. To create a road, the same path has to be passed many times. The process of creating a road or memory depends a lot on the conditions in which cart is moving. That means that there are people capable of remembering most of the text just after two readings. How can they do that? In the text below, I will mention some of the best-known techniques used to improve memory. By the way, if a road can be created in the wet soil after only three passes, why even bother to ride over dry ground? :) It is only a matter of creating optimal conditions and using appropriate techniques that facilitate the process of learning and memory.

Which factors influence our memory?

There are several ways to improve our memory. In general, it means changing several living habits.

You should:
– eat healthy;
– exercise. Sport and physical activity lead to better concentration and therefore to better memory;
– get your emotions, spirit and mind in balance;
– reduce stress;
– make sure that you have a good night sleep;
– avoid alcohol and other harmful substances.

Also, learning foreign languages, listening to music and socializing help our brain have better memory. Various studies showed that developing and nurturing good friendships, as well as finding new contacts causes increase in brain capacity and therefore a better memory. That makes sense. Through new impulses and stimuli, these processes help the brain develop.

Advices for easier and more efficient memory

In order to be able to use your time in the most efficient way you should follow a few useful advices. You probably had an experience of reading a material that was easy to remember, your progress was quick and afterwards you were satisfied with the amount of material you learned. On the other hand, you probably had situations when you were unable to progress besides putting in a great effort. There are several factors that helped me, which I hope you will find useful too.

1. Effects of motivation to the memory process

Did you know that on average a man uses only 10% of its memory? Many readers face the problem of losing motivation during reading. Due to circumstances we are often forced to read literature we are not particularly interested in. Job or the need to acquire new skills require us to improve and develop our knowledge in specific segment. If this segment however is not something we are particularly interested in, we often have the problem of lack of motivation. It is a well-known fact that it is much harder to do things that we have to do than it is to indulge into a new hobby. There are many books about motivation, so I will not write a lot on this subject. If you face a difficult task that requires a lot of work, try to split the work into several stages. I advise you to make an Excel table that will contain the following items:

– goal;
– why I want to accomplish this goal?

— which positive results I can expect after I complete the task?
— obstacles I have to overcome.

The idea is to develop an elaborate plan and give detailed description of positive results. If you explain your goal in more beautiful and meaningful way the problem of motivation will become significantly smaller. It is much easier to motivate yourself and to work when you have a clear goal and when you have developed practical steps towards accomplishing it. It is also useful to define deadlines by which parts of the task have to be completed. As an additional encouragement, I suggest that you make a separate Excel sheet titled "My record". The idea is that you measure how many minutes each day you have spent on working towards your goal. This graphic representation can give you a great overview of the time spent. For example, if you see that on Wednesday two weeks ago you spent entire three hours on achieving your goal, you will be additionally motivated to break that record. A useful and in my opinion positive attitude towards achieving the goals you set.

By the way, everyone has different ways of motivating themselves. If it works, keep on using it. It is useful to give yourself a small reward after completing a task. It can be in the form of your favourite fruit, a spoon of honey, 15 minutes rest, listening to your favourite song, any activity you like. You can look at this as a reward for a job well done.

In short, if you approach a task with higher motivation your memory will be better.

2. Clarity, comprehension and its impact on memory

Let's say you are looking at a text written in Chinese or any other foreign language. What are your chances of memorizing such text? Probably equal to zero. You can conclude that our level of comprehension during reading plays a huge part in the memory process. The lower level of comprehension is, the worse the memory. If, as mentioned in the example above, level of comprehension is equal to zero, then the memory has the same value. The goal when you read a text is to improve comprehension level, i.e. understanding.

This technique can help you do that.
a) create a summary of the material you are about to read.
By this I mean going through several pages you are about to read. Spend at least a few seconds on each page. Read the headings, subheadings, bold text, graphs and prominent details. In this way you develop a rough idea about the text.
b) read the entire text you planned;
c) reread the text.
It is best to reread the text one day after the initial reading. With each new reading the text becomes clearer and after a few days you will notice that you have better comprehension and memory of the material.

By the way, did you know that some of the best students don't even use markers to highlight text when they study? They only read the textbook every day with understanding. After reading it for a certain number of times, the entire sentences and paragraphs become memorized. When I attended high school, I loved reading Tolkien. Lord of the Rings was my favourite book. I remember how I read this 1000-page book four times in one year. In time I discovered that I was able to quote entire paragraphs or pages without looking at the book. I knew every event, fact or date. So, your memory will get more detailed with every reread. Avoid rote learning whenever you can. Such knowledge often lasts very shortly and gest forgotten very quickly.

3. Finding logic in the text we read

The memory process also depends on logic and the way in which we sort our thought. Let's look at these three series of numbers, for example:
5+9=65
3+5=12
1+8=7
In order to remember these three lines, you have to remember three groups of numbers in each line. Since results are wrong, it is not enough to remember just two lines, but you have to remember all the numbers. In order to memorize this, in this example we are battling an illogical scenario. We know that equations are incorrect, but we have to memorize them. This causes discontent. This type of learning often results in slow progress. On the other hand, it is much easier to memorize information if it is logical and meaningful.

Let's look at the following numbers:
3+3=6
6+6=12
12+12=24

There is a clear logic and you just have to remember the number 3. The rest of the numbers follow a clear pattern that is easily memorized. You can find similar examples in texts. You should always try to find the main, i.e. basic idea of the author and the logic behind it. Once you find it, it will become much easier to memorize, the same as in the example with the numbers.

4. Better memory by developing a map of key words

Mind maps have been used for centuries but have become popular through TV lectures of Tony Buzan.
His book - "Mind Maps" - was first published in 1997 and since then this concept has become very popular. This method includes creating associations and connections between key words and the main subject. Table of contents in a book can be seem as a sort of a mind map. For example, this book contains four main parts.

Mind Map Example:

Speed Reading	about speed reading
	necessary conditions
	theoretical part
	exercises

Also, you can extend each of the segments by new key words:

Theoretical part	bad habits
	aids
	text complexity
	higher comprehension
	reading by segments
	comprehension test
	advanced techniques

A material rearranged in this way is much clearer and therefore easier to learn and remember.

It is recommended to decorate these maps in different colours, by using different fonts in order to make them more appealing and interesting. When you complete a map and decorate it, it will be much easier to remember different segments of the text.

5. Autosuggestion and its impact on memory

Autosuggestion is a powerful tool. A lot of books have been written on this subject and for a good reason. If you are facing difficult and large reading assignment that you find very hard to complete, try improving your chances by saying the following lines:

I like working on...
The more time I spend doing ..... the better I get.
In time I will become expert in ....
The material I read is actually very interesting and useful when you look at it from this perspective.
I am happy that I will be able to do everything I have planned for today.

The autosuggestion improves your concentration level and indirectly leads to better memory.

6. The effects of positive attitude on better memory

Tony Robbins put an excellent perspective on the way emotions affect us, our everyday life and activities. The book Principle of Power is a great take on this subject. In short, people are prone to attach an abundance of bad emotions to every hard and time-consuming tasks. Therefore, when we are engaged in such activity, we are burdened by bad emotions. The main idea is to gradually, step by step, replace the bad emotions with positive, thus making the task easier. Having a positive attitude during learning and memorizing will help you progress much faster.

7. **Persistence as a proven way of consolidating the memory**

Long-term memory often depends on the frequency certain thought is retrieved. The example of cart and meadow can be applied here also. In the beginning the terrain was uneven and covered in bushes, and later it developed into passable and regulated road. Persistence plays a key part here. In practice, the more times we repeat a certain thought and retrieve it, the better we will remember it. The best effects of long-term memory are achieved when we read a text that we understand. Repeating and rereading after longer periods of time is very important.

There is a Chinese saying:

The man who moved a mountain was the one who began carrying away small stones.

8. Visualisation and attaching emotions significantly help memory

The concept of visual memory was unknown to me before I started getting interested into books on that topic. This concept was frequently mentioned in many books I read. In the beginning I didn't pay much attention to it before I tried the technique for myself. You can see how powerful this method of memory is on the following example about learning foreign words.

Let's say you set yourself a goal of learning a dictionary that has 70.000 foreign words. If you try to simply learn it by heart, that will quickly cause frustration and you will progress very slowly. However, if you try and picture a foreign word, memory becomes better.

Let's say you hear the word "collapse" for the first time in the language you are learning. Simple mechanical learning or rote learning will not help you quickly memorize it. If, on the other hand, you picture yourself **collapsing** through a wooden floor of a pit toilet, grasping for slippery and rotten wooden planks that fell through together with you into the sewer - the chances of forgetting this word are close to none. If you add the specific smell associated with such place, your state of shock caused by unbelievable and unexpected accident, you will most certainly remember this word.

So, the next time you hear the word "collapsing" it will certainly bring the image of a pit toilet, rotten planks and the right word. Interesting, isn't it? :)

This concept of visualisation can successfully be applied to many foreign words and makes memory much easier. The reason lies in visualisation and adding emotions to the picture. Just remember that more unbelievable or stranger situations help the idea to get more easily stuck into your memory.

9. Useful trick for better memory

Certain studies about memory resulted in this discovery. Rapid eye movement from left to right can lead to better memory. This exercise lasts about 30 seconds and is can be seen as a way to stretch your brain.

Summary:

— keep motivation and concentration at the highest possible level;
— try to understand the text you are reading;
— make logical connections between events and contents;
— make a map of key words to have better overview of the material you are studying;
— try to make a text more interesting by using autosuggestion and positive attitude;
— regularly repeat the text you are learning until you are sure you have memorized well;
— use the visualisation system.

In the end of this chapter, I would like to share with you a couple of interesting quotes on memory:

"The advantage of a bad memory is that one enjoys several times the same good things for the first time."
Friedrich Nietzsche

„I remember the things I want to forget, but don't forget those I want to forget."
Euripides

„Life - it is not about the days that have passed, but about those we remembered."
Pyotr Andreyevich Pavlenko

„The best memory training:
Lend money to somebody."
Prof. Dr. Hans-Jürgen Quadbeck-Seeger

The Journal of Achieved Results and for Progress Tracking

You can use this page to track your progress. I suggest that you test yourself every 30 days and write the results below. You should always use new, unknown text for a new test. If you read the same text several times in a row, you will not get correct results.

Date of the first text: _____
Achieved speed: _____

Date of the first text: _____
Achieved speed: _____

Date of the first text: _____
Achieved speed: _____

Date of the first text: _____
Achieved speed: _____

Date of the first text: _____
Achieved speed: _____

Date of the first text: _____
Achieved speed: _____

Date of the first text: _____
Achieved speed: _____

Date of the first text: _____
Achieved speed: _____

Date of the first text: _____
Achieved speed: _____

Date of the first text: _____
Achieved speed: _____

Date of the first text: _____
Achieved speed: _____

Date of the first text: _____
Achieved speed: _____

Date of the first text: _____
Achieved speed: _____

Date of the first text: _____
Achieved speed: _____

Date of the first text: _____
Achieved speed: _____

Date of the first text: _____
Achieved speed: _____

Date of the first text: _____
Achieved speed: _____

Date of the first text: _____
Achieved speed: _____

Author's afterword

Dear readers,
I hope that this book helped you and that you are now reading faster than you used to before. If you are satisfied with its contents and quality, feel free to recommend it to your friends and leave a short review on the website where you bought it.

I will be very happy to hear your impressions about speed reading and the results you achieved.

Thank you once again for buying this book.

Stefan Krneta

Literature:

Tony Buzan: The Speed Reading Book, BBC Active 2009

Wofgang Schmitz, Friedrich Hasse, Britta Sosemann: Schneller lesen – besser verstehen, Rowohlt Taschenbuch Verlag 2016

Günther Koch: Speed Reading fürs Studium, Ferdinand Schöningh GmbH & Co. KG 2015

Ernst Ott: Optimales Lesen - schneller lesen mehr behalten, Nikol Verlagsgesellschaft 2016

Birgit Kuhn: Lesetechniken optimieren - schneller lesen, leichter merken, Compact Verlag GmbH 2016

Geoffrey A. Dudley: The High-Speed Way to Increase Your Learning Power

Adler, Mortimer J./van Doren, Charles: How to read a Book, Touchstone Books 1972

Dehaene Stanislas: Lesen. Die größte Erfindung der Menschheit und was dabei in unseren Köpfen passiert, München 2010

Viktor Medvedev: How to improve eyesight, Infostudio 2014

Pritzel, Monika/Brand, Matthias/Markowitsch, Hans J. : Gehirn und Verhalten. Ein Grandkurs der physiologischen Psychologie, Heidelberg 2009

Ralph Radach: Blickbewegungen beim Lesen: Psychologische Aspekte der Determination von Fixationspositionen, Münster, New York 1996

Gerhard Roth: Bildung braucht Persönlichkeit: Wie Lernen gelingt, Stuttgart 2011

Cutler Wade: Triple Your Reading Speed, Pocket Books 2003

Nila Banton Smith: Speed Reading Made Easy, Warner Books 1992

Stanley D. Frank: Remember Everything You Read: The Evelyn Wood 7-Day Speed Reading & Learning Program, Avon 1992

Graham King: The Secrets of Speed Reading, Mandarin 1993

Thomas Grabner: Speed Reading: Sofort schneller Lesen und mehr verstehen!, CreateSpace 2017

Tim Winter: Speed Reading: Wie Sie mit Speed Reading sofort Ihre Lesegeschwindigkeit verdoppeln, schneller lesen und verstehen werden, CreateSpace 2017

Mark Licz: Speed Reading für Studenten: Schneller lesen und begreifen: die Turbotechnik zur besseren Note, CreateSpace 2015

Norman C. Maberly: Mastering Speed Reading, Signet 1966
Georgij Nazarov: Tajne čišćenja mozga : kako povećati sposobnosti mozga bez obzira na životno doba?, Esotheria 2008

99 Tatsachen über Ihr Gedächtnis: Wie es funktioniert - Was es leistet - Wie Sie es schützen und stärken

Hans Förstl, Barbara Knab, Karin Baum

Gedächtnis verbessern: Wie Du Dein Gedächtnis und Deine Konzentration durch Gehirnjogging steigern kannst, Richard Bachmeier

https://sr.wikipedia.org/sr-el/%D0%9F%D0%B0%D0%BC%D1%9B%D0%B5%D1%9A%D0%B5
https://sr.wikipedia.org/sr-el/%D0%9F%D0%B0%D0%BC%D1%9B%D0%B5%D1%9A%D0%B5
https://de.wikipedia.org/wiki/Ged%C3%A4chtnis#Langzeitged%C3%A4chtnis

Text about u Don Quixote taken from the page:
https://sr.wikipedia.org/sr-el/%D0%94%D0%BE%D0%BD_%D0%9A%D0%B8%D1%85%D0%BE%D1%82

Human Memory
http://www.human-memory.net/types.html

Text about penguins taken from the page:
https://sr.wikipedia.org/sr-el/%D0%9F%D0%B8%D0%BD%D0%B3%D0%B2%D0%B8%D0%BD

Text about speed reading tests taken from the page:
https://de.wikipedia.org/wiki/Schnelllesen

Disclaimer

The material for this book was prepared with great care. However, we cannot claim that information contained herein are correct, complete and up-to-date or take any responsibility arising from such claim. Information contained herein represents a personal opinion of the author, which he developed from many years of experience and research. For this reason, the author does not assume any legal liability for damages caused as a result of mistake or improper understanding of contents by a reader. This book is a guideline, which allows you to achieve success more easily, but there are no guarantees that you will achieve such success. For this reason, the author cannot be held liable if you fail to achieve the goals set.

Notes

Made in the USA
Thornton, CO
04/20/23 17:13:55

29b84cfc-0cf1-4a0b-98f2-3bf68aa9323fR02